Early in the Sixties the idealistic young joined hands to abolish injustice and fight the inequities and evils of society. Dedicated to nonviolence they sang "We Shall Overcome," launched sit-ins and peaceful protests. They listened fervently to their idols, the Kennedy brothers, Martin Luther King, Malcolm X, Medgar Evers.

By the end of the decade the idols were all dead. The Student Nonviolent Coordinating Committee had changed its name—and its tactics. A president had been driven from office and the nation's campuses and ghettos were rocked by bloody violence. All over the country people were asking, "Why? How did it happen? What do they really want?"

Helene Hanff attempts to answer these questions. Her movers and shakers are the involved young, caught up in a true moral revolution, exposing and challenging the corruptions of the established system. She believes they are "the most gallant, undiscouragable and remarkable young generation this country has ever produced." She dedicates this book to them, and addresses it to the up-and-coming generation of the Seventies—the youth who may now become the new movers and shakers of America.

OTHER BOOKS BY HELENE HANFF ARE:

ADULT

Underfoot in Show Business

JUVENILE

Terrible Thomas
Butch Elects a Mayor
The Day They Signed the Constitution
The Battle for New Orleans
The Unlikely Twins
John F. Kennedy, Young Man of Destiny
Our Nation's Capital
Mexico
Religious Freedom in America
The Early Settlers
The Good Neighbour
Elizabeth I of England

the movers and shakers

The Young Activists of the Sixties

HELENE HANFF

S. G. Phillips *New York*

323
H238m

SECOND PRINTING, 1971

We are the music-makers,
And we are the dreamers of dreams,
Wandering by lone sea-breakers,
And sitting by desolate streams;
World-losers and world-forsakers,
On whom the pale moon gleams:
Yet we are the movers and shakers
Of the world forever, it seems.
From: *Ode* by Arthur W. E. O'Shaughnessy

CONTENTS

ILLUSTRATIONS

GLOSSARY
OF ORGANIZATIONS

Since most of the organizations mentioned are referred to by
their initials more often than by their full titles, the following
list of titles and abbreviations is included for easy reference.

CIA	Central Intelligence Agency
COFO	Council of Freedom Organizations
CORE	Congress of Racial Equality
FBI	Federal Bureau of Investigation
FSM	Free Speech Movement
IDA	Institute for Defense Analyses
NAACP	National Association for the Advancement of Colored People
NSA	National Student Association
ROTC	Reserve Officers' Training Corps
SANE	National Committee for a Sane Nuclear Policy
SAS	Students' Afro-American Society
SCLC	Southern Christian Leadership Conference
SDS	Students for a Democratic Society
SEEK	Search for Education, Evaluation, and Knowledge
SNCC (Snick)	Students' National Coordinating Committee (formerly Students' Nonviolent Coordinating Committee)
YIP (Yippies)	Youth International Party

the
movers
and
shakers

APOLOGIA:
How This Book Came to be Written

It is a strange fact that each decade of the twentieth century seems to have had a separate, sharply defined image. From the Trust-Busting Nineteen Hundreds and the Suffragette-and-Prohibition Teens, on through the Jazz-Age Twenties, the Depression Thirties, and the War Forties, each decade took on its own individual character. The Affluent Fifties were no exception.

Politically, the Fifties were known as the Era of McCarthyism, an era dominated less by the Eisenhower administration than by the anti-Communist investigations of the late Senator Joseph McCarthy. It was a time in which scientists, educators, actors, and writers were fired from their jobs, blacklisted by their professional establishments, and frequently imprisoned for political activities in which they had legally engaged twenty years before. In such an atmosphere, a blanket of fear and silence settled over the country.

Nowhere was this silence more profound than on college campuses. Students saw their professors dismissed from their jobs without trial, often without knowing the charges against them or the names of their accusers. To protect itself against a similar fate, the college generation of the Fifties withdrew into a "cool," detached world. Their credo was self-preservation through careful noninvolvement: "Don't join anything, don't sign anything, don't criticize anything, don't get involved."

"The employers will love this generation," remarked President Clark Kerr of the University of California at Berkeley,

13

in 1959. "They aren't going to press any grievances. They are going to be easy to handle. There aren't going to be any riots."

But Clark Kerr was speaking of a generation about to graduate its final class. Nine-tenths of the Silent Generation had already graduated and disappeared into the establishment corporations, ad agencies, and law firms of the Affluent Fifties. A new decade was about to open, bringing with it a new young generation, which within five years would drive Kerr himself out of office.

Nevertheless, the Fifties had produced a few young men with the courage to speak out against the evils of the American establishment. One of these was a twenty-seven-year-old minister named Martin Luther King, Jr. who, in 1954 and 1955, led a Negro bus boycott in Montgomery, Alabama, to win for his people the elementary right to sit where they pleased on a public bus. Two years later, in 1957, Dr. King founded the Southern Christian Leadership Conference (SCLC), composed of young black activists like himself. Together they began to map a plan for obtaining rights for the Negro which, though guaranteed by the U.S. Constitution and many U.S. laws, were denied in practice.

In the last century, for example, the Supreme Court had ruled that the South might maintain separate schools for blacks and whites provided that the schools were equal. This "separate but equal" law had never been obeyed by the South; Southern white and black schools were so brutally unequal as to make a comparison between them grotesque. When in 1954 the Supreme Court reversed the "separate but equal" ruling and ordered the nation's schools integrated, the law was once again ignored throughout the country. By 1959, Southern schools were being desegregated at the rate of one percent a year. Northern schools, segregated automatically since they existed in all-white or all-black neighborhoods, were desegregating no faster.

General and casual lawbreaking as the Fifties closed was by no means confined to the area of Civil Rights. As the country grew daily richer, more powerful, and more complacent, its political, military, economic, and industrial establishments were growing daily more corrupt. People joked about corruption in government, corruption in labor and industry, corruption in the courts, while continuing to mouth the time-honored clichés about all men being equal in this just and free republic. If this national hypocrisy was largely unconscious, it was nevertheless all-pervasive. The country was too prosperous and too comfortable on the whole to be seriously disturbed by its own growing immorality. A small segment of the younger generation of the Fifties—known as "the Beat Generation," or "Beatniks"—was profoundly shocked by this immorality. But condemning American society out of hand, these alienated young people chose to live apart from it rather than make any effort to change it.

Came 1960—and as if a curtain had been rung up, a new and revolutionary decade exploded, dominated by a new young generation. Like the Beatniks before them—like the young rebels of every generation—the activists of the Sixties were a small minority of their generation; yet this small minority was to dominate the decade. Instead of withdrawing from society, the young activists of the Sixties set out to reform it.

Beginning in 1960 and continuing without letup through 1969, they launched a series of movements, each of which had as its goal the reformation of a corrupt establishment. The chief targets were the segregationist establishment, the military establishment, the political establishment, and the academic establishment. This unity of moral purpose drove the young leaders of one movement to become followers in one or more of the other movements. In so doing, they doubled and redoubled their own suffering.

15

The young of the Sixties were to be clubbed, beaten, and gassed by state and local police in the South and by military police at the Pentagon. They were to be imprisoned by Southern sheriffs and Northern and Western draft boards; they were to be saddled with criminal police records by university administrations throughout the country. In their battle to help black Southerners gain the simplest rights of American citizenship, many young people were to be murdered in cold blood.

Each movement had its leaders who sprang briefly into prominence; but for the most part, the movements created their leaders, overshadowed them, and moved on without them when necessary. And it was often necessary. For in challenging the establishment—even in challenging it to enforce its own laws—the young activists were to find the power of the country arrayed against them. Each nonviolent movement was to see one leader after another cut down by assassin's bullets. In a decade marked by unprecedented violence and bloodshed, it is important to note that the violence never came from the youthful reformers. It came invariably from the establishment they sought to reform. Not until the final year of the Sixties did a few of the young activists fight back in kind.

Through it all, the young people were consistently denounced by most of the nation's press, by many national leaders, and by almost all of middle-aged America. This author, being middle-aged, was among those who condemned them, judging them by what the news media reported of their activities.

It was while doing research for what was planned as a wholly different book that the author slowly uncovered the facts of the youthful movements of the Sixties, facts which the average citizen lacked the time and means to discover. Slowly, and with a growing sense of incredulity, the author discovered that what she had heard, read, and believed about the young activists—about their attempts to "destroy" and "tear down"

American institutions through "rioting" and "violence"—was not true. The more facts the author uncovered, the more she was forced to revise her early judgment, until at length she abandoned the book originally planned and decided to write the present volume instead. The limited time and even more limited research facilities available make it necessary to apologize for the many errors and omissions with which the book may fairly be charged; some omissions in particular require an additional explanation.

Since this volume is devoted to those movements of young people which set out to reform existing establishments, several important groups—all of which had an undoubted influence on their own generation and an impact on the Sixties—have been omitted as not properly falling within the limits of this book.

For example, the hippies, spiritual heirs to the Beatniks, have been omitted because they too chose to withdraw from society rather than attempt to reform it. The Yippies were not included because it seems to this author that they never achieved the purpose or size of a genuine movement. A few Yippies worked in SNCC. All of them became part of the antiwar movement. But as a separate entity, the Yippies made no contribution uniquely their own, beyond their rather self-conscious, satiric style.

Most serious is the omission of the Black Panthers. They were left out partly because they constitute not a movement but an attempt to found a new political party. Even so, since the Panthers were unquestionably among the youthful reformers of the Sixties, their story would have been included had it been possible at present writing to obtain factual, reliable, reasonably unbiased information about them sufficient to tell their story.

With all its imperfections, this book will serve its purpose if it conveys to the reader a sense of the moral commitment, the remarkable achievements, and the appalling courage of the young crusaders of the Sixties. For it is in the belief that their reforming zeal constitutes the best hope for their country's future that this book has been written about—and is dedicated to—the gallant members of all the young movements of the Sixties.

1

SNCC vs.
THE SEGREGATIONIST ESTABLISHMENT

On Sunday evening, January 31, 1960, four freshmen were holding a bull session in a dormitory room at North Carolina Agricultural and Technical College, a Negro college outside Greensboro, North Carolina. The subject of the bull session was a situation which, as one of the students put it later, "just didn't seem right."

Week in and week out, they walked two miles into Greensboro to buy notebooks, paper, pens, toothpaste, soap, and shaving cream at the local Woolworth's, but they could not sit down for a cup of coffee at the lunch counter before the long walk back to college. The Woolworth lunch counter, like all lunch counters in the South in 1960, was "for whites only." Discussing the situation that night, the boys decided to do something about it.

On the following day—February 1, 1960—the four boys walked to Greensboro, went into Woolworth's, and bought toothpaste. Then they crossed the aisle, sat down at the lunch counter, and ordered coffee. As described by Jack Newfield in *A Prophetic Minority,* the waitress was polite.

"I'm sorry," she said, "but we don't serve Negroes here."

"I beg your pardon, but you just served me at a counter two feet away," one of the boys contradicted politely. Why, he asked, was it all right to serve him at one counter but not at another?

The waitress had no answer. She did not serve the students and they did not leave. They sat at the counter, unserved, until the store closed. Then they went home.

A lunch counter sit-in. *CORE*

The next day they were back, with friends. Again the waitress refused to serve them; again they sat until the store closed. Of course, by occupying seats without being served they were cutting into the lunch counter's business. On Wednesday, when a larger group of students arrived, they were thrown out bodily by the manager. On Friday they were back, so many of them this time that they occupied all the seats at the counter and found there weren't enough to go around. The boys who couldn't find seats at Woolworth's moved up the street to Kress's a block away and sat at the counter there. Sit-ins had begun, and with them a new movement.

The Sit-ins

Sit-ins were not new. They had been tried back in the 1940's by the National Association for the Advancement of Colored People (NAACP) and in the 1950's by the Congress of Racial Equality (CORE), but only in isolated cities and as the result of careful planning. Not until the Greensboro college students sat in in February of 1960 did the technique suddenly catch fire, growing with incredible rapidity. Conducted entirely by college students, without organization or direction, the sit-in movement spread within a few days to seven South Carolina cities serving nearby Negro colleges. In two weeks it had expanded to fifteen cities in five Southern states.

In Raleigh, North Carolina, black students were joined by white students, and on February 12, Lincoln's Birthday, forty-three integrated sit-inners became the first to be arrested.

In Orangeburg, South Carolina, student sit-ins that same month resulted in the swift closing of lunch counters in the downtown business district. This galvanized the two nearby Negro college campuses, and a thousand students marched in protest through the streets of the city. In mid-March, the lunch counters reopened—and a fresh wave of sit-ins began, supported by another peaceful march. This time, the police moved in with tear gas and fire hoses. Over five hundred students were arrested. The local jail was not big enough to hold them, and three hundred and fifty of the students were herded into an eight-foot-high open-air chicken coop. It began to rain; and packed in the barbed-wire coop in the cold March rain, the students held a prayer meeting and sang the Star-Spangled Banner.

In Nashville, Tennessee, black and white students from Negro Fisk and white Vanderbilt universities sat in together at a lunch counter, just a few weeks after the Greensboro incident. They sat patiently and without complaint as white segregationist hecklers jabbed the necks of the girls with lighted cigarettes, and knocked a Vanderbilt student off his counter stool to the floor and beat him.

The students did not fight back, then or at any time in the history of the movement. Ranging in age from fifteen to twenty-one, they displayed a courage and a dignity few adults could have matched under such conditions. Thanks largely to the impact upon them of Malcolm X's words and Martin Luther King's actions, these young black Americans were a different breed from the generations of Negroes who had preceded them—a new look noted ruefully by the *Richmond News Leader* in a Washington's Birthday editorial prompted by Richmond sit-ins.

"Many a Virginian must have felt a tinge of wry regret at the state of things as they are, reading of Saturday's 'sit-downs' by Negro students in Richmond stores. Here were the colored students, in coats, white shirts, ties, and one of them was reading Goethe and one was taking notes from a biology text. And here, on the sidewalk outside, was a gang of white boys come to heckle, a ragtail rabble, slack-jawed, black-jacketed, grinning fit to kill . . . waving the proud and honored flag of the Southern States. . . . It gives one pause."

None of this was lost on Dr. King's SCLC. Ella Baker, SCLC's executive secretary, felt that the student movement needed adult organization and direction. She wrote to student leaders in Negro colleges throughout the South, inviting them to a conference to be held at Shaw University in Raleigh over the Easter weekend.

On April 15, black and white students began arriving at Shaw not only from all over the Deep South, from Tennessee, Kentucky, and Virginia, but from nineteen white colleges in the North as well. Of the two hundred people assembled for the conference, one hundred twenty-six were students. Among them was a twenty-year-old Atlanta student named Julian Bond, who later described the nonstudents who attended:

"People from SCLC, CORE, the NAACP . . . were at the meeting. Some of them wanted to make the sit-in leaders the nucleus of a youth arm of the SCLC. Others wanted us to become CORE chapters. The NAACP thought we could raise money for them."

But the young students had a sense of their own mission and their own identity. That weekend they politely but firmly declined to become a junior wing of any existing organization. They would instead found an organization of their own, aided and advised by the older groups.

The new organization was christened the Students' Nonviolent Coordinating Committee—SNCC—and its young members almost at once dubbed it "Snick." A month after the founding conference at Shaw, a black Vanderbilt divinity student, James Lawson, wrote SNCC's Statement of Purpose.

"We affirm the philosophical or religious ideal of nonviolence as the foundation of our purpose . . . and the manner of our action," ran the document. "Through nonviolence, courage displaces fear; love transcends hate . . . peace dominates war . . . justice . . . overthrows injustice."

Thus was SNCC born in an idealistic commitment to nonviolence, love, peace, and justice. The segregationist establishment was to answer with bombs, fire, imprisonment, and murder.

Of those first few months of SNCC sit-ins, Howard Zinn, in *SNCC, The New Abolitionists,* wrote:

"In Jacksonville, Florida . . . a white sit-in student was attacked in jail and his jaw was broken; a sixteen-year-old Negro boy was pistol-whipped by the Ku Klux Klan; a Negro man unconnected with the demonstrations . . . was shot to death by a white service-station attendant. In Atlanta, acid was thrown at sit-in leader Lonnie King. In Frankfort, Kentucky, the gymnasium of a Negro college was set afire. In Columbia, South Carolina, a Negro sit-in was stabbed. In Houston, Texas, a twenty-seven-year-old Negro was kidnapped and flogged with a chain, and the symbol KKK was carved on his chest. . . . When students marched down the street in Jackson (Mississippi), police used clubs, tear gas, and police dogs. In Biloxi, Mississippi, Negroes trying to use a public beach were attacked with clubs and chains by crowds of whites, and ten were wounded by gunfire."

Hundreds of students were arrested for sitting in, and sentenced to terms ranging from a month in the local jail to two years in state reformatories. In Georgia, a black college student was sentenced to two years on a chain gang for the crime of asking for a cup of coffee at Woolworth's.

Expulsion from Southern colleges was another form of reprisal against students who took part in sit-ins. For his actions in drafting SNCC's Statement of Purpose, and for teaching classes in nonviolent techniques, James Lawson was expelled from Vanderbilt University three months before he was to graduate. (Though all sixteen members of the Divinity School faculty were white, eleven of them resigned in protest at Lawson's expulsion.)

Such a reprisal might have been expected from a Southern white college such as Vanderbilt. What shocked SNCC students was the speed with which Negro presidents of state-owned Southern Negro colleges acted against students who were challenging the segregation status quo. That spring of

1960, under pressure from the white state legislators who appointed them, Negro college administrators in Georgia, Alabama, Florida, and Louisiana expelled students for participating in sit-ins and for picketing stores which practiced segregation.

Despite reprisals, SNCC continued to attract increasing numbers of student volunteers, black and white, and the sit-ins spread throughout the South. Chain stores which continued to refuse service to black students after a week or two of sit-ins found more than their lunch-counter business affected: student picket lines and word-of-mouth urged black families to boycott the chain stores which depended heavily on them for patronage.

At the same time, Northern college students who had taken up the SNCC cause began to apply pressure by picketing chain stores which practiced segregation in their Southern branches. A collegiate picket line outside Woolworth's in New York or Boston, informing the public that the store excluded black patrons from its lunch counters in the South, was an acute embarrassment to the chain store as well as an additional economic threat.

In city after city, as the pressures mounted, Woolworth's, Kress's, and other chain stores capitulated. Before the end of 1961, lunch counters were desegregated throughout the border states of Arkansas, Tennessee, Texas, and Oklahoma, and in such major Southern cities as Richmond and Atlanta. As Howard Zinn observed, "Men and women seeking a sandwich at a lunch counter . . . were more interested in satisfying their hunger or their thirst than in who sat next to them. After two months of desegregation in Winston-Salem, North Carolina, the manager of a large store said, 'You would think it had been going on for fifty years. I am tickled to death over the situation.'"

Only in Mississippi and the rural areas of Louisiana, Georgia, South Carolina, and Alabama did the sit-ins fail to

Freedom Riders leaving Washington, D.C., for the South. *CORE*

make a crack in the wall of segregation. Wrote Ralph McGill in *The South and the Southerner:*

"The sit-ins were, without question, productive of the most change. . . . They inspired adult men and women, fathers, mothers, grandmothers, aunts, and uncles, to support the young students."

But for SNCC, the sit-ins were only the beginning.

The Freedom Rides

In 1961, the Interstate Commerce Commission ruled that segregation, which had long been illegal on interstate buses, was illegal in bus terminals as well. The decision was ignored throughout the South, where bus terminals continued to display illegal "white" and "colored" signs over separate sections of waiting rooms and washrooms.

It was to test Southern obedience to the new law that CORE, in May of 1961, launched the famous Freedom Rides. Enlisting the help of SNCC students, CORE organized groups of black and white riders to board buses together and ride through the South, disembarking at Southern terminals where they would ignore the "white" and "colored" signs, entering the waiting rooms in integrated groups.

On May 4, the first two groups of Freedom Riders boarded a Greyhound and a Trailways bus in Washington, D. C., ready to ride through the South to New Orleans. SNCC volunteer John Lewis, a black seminary student who had taken part in the Nashville sit-ins, was one of the riders on the Greyhound bus. When the bus reached the terminal in Rock Hill, South Carolina, Lewis had the dubious distinction of being the first Freedom Rider to be set upon and beaten by a band of white segregationists.

The two buses rolled on without further incident, however, and by May 13 had made it safely to Atlanta. It was when they crossed into Alabama that the trouble erupted. On May

14—Mother's Day—the Greyhound bus arrived at Anniston, Alabama, to find a white mob waiting for it just outside of town. The mob surrounded the bus and hurled a "Molotov cocktail," setting the bus on fire. The Freedom Riders escaped as the bus went up in flames and they boarded another bus for Birmingham. Meanwhile, when the Trailways bus arrived at the Anniston station, eight white men boarded it, attacked and beat two of the black Freedom Riders, and forced all the black Freedom Riders to move to the back of the bus before permitting the driver to proceed.

At Birmingham, the Freedom Riders disembarked and entered the "white" waiting room, where a mob attacked them with baseball bats and iron bars. A band of white men attacked CORE leader Jim Peck and a SNCC volunteer from Atlanta University, working them over with fists and iron pipes, leaving Peck unconscious in an alleyway with a gash in his head which required fifty-three stitches. Birmingham's notorious police chief, "Bull" Connor, explained to newsmen that he had been unable to offer police protection because it was Mother's Day and his men had the day off. Fearful of the vengeance of the mob, Birmingham bus drivers refused to take the Freedom Riders on the last lap of their journey. The ride ended in Birmingham, and the Freedom Riders took a plane on to New Orleans.

This news reached other SNCC students, and angered them. On May 18, four days after the Mother's Day fiasco, a group of black and white SNCC students boarded a Greyhound bus at Nashville and headed for Birmingham, determined to ride on to New Orleans during the next week. As they disembarked at the Birmingham terminal they were taken into "protective custody" by the police and put in jail overnight.

Early the next morning, "Bull" Connor drove the Freedom Riders one hundred and twenty miles to the Tennessee border and dumped them there. Eight hours later he found them back

May 14, 1961: Freedom Riders watch as their Greyhound bus goes up in flames near Anniston, Alabama. *UPI*

May 28, 1961: Freedom Riders sit in the "white only" section of the Montgomery, Alabama, Trailways bus terminal. *CORE*

in the Birmingham terminal. They had walked from the Tennessee border to Nashville and promptly boarded another bus for Birmingham.

No bus driver, however, could be found to take them from Birmingham on to Montgomery. ("I have only one life to give," one bus driver is quoted as telling a young coed, "and I'm not going to give it to NAACP or CORE!") All night the students waited in the bus terminal. At dawn, a bus driver collecting tickets for the Montgomery run found only a few white reporters boarding his bus and decided it was safe to take the Freedom Riders aboard.

On Saturday, May 20, the bus arrived at Montgomery. Government representatives were on hand to meet it. One of these was John Siegenthaler, aide to Attorney General Robert F. Kennedy, who had flown to Montgomery to confer with Governor Patterson. The governor had assured him that there was no need for federal intervention to guarantee the safety of any bus rider in Alabama. Waiting for the Freedom Riders with Siegenthaler and the other government representatives were several TV cameramen and newspaper reporters, and a crowd of about three hundred whites.

Twenty or thirty of the mob pounced first on the newsmen, beating them and smashing their photographic equipment. Then they fell on the Freedom Riders, attacking them with iron pipes, clubs, and sticks.

SNCC volunteer James Zwerg, a white student from Wisconsin, was knocked down by a group of white teen-agers and beaten and stomped while white women watching shouted, "Kill the nigger-loving son-of-a-bitch!" Another white woman, spotting two Negroes standing in front of the terminal watching the scene, shouted "Get those niggers!"—and the mob set on the two men, though neither was a Freedom Rider. John Lewis was beaten as he lay on the ground with blood running from his mouth. Not until twenty-two people had been injured

—including four newsmen and John Siegenthaler—did the police arrive to disperse the mob with tear gas.

The riders stayed in Montgomery four days, as guests in Negro homes, until the injured among them were able to travel. On Wednesday, May 24, accompanied by National Guardsmen and sixteen reporters, they left Montgomery for Jackson, with James Lawson holding classes in nonviolent techniques on the bus as it rode into Mississippi.

At Jackson, twenty-seven Freedom Riders were arrested and given the choice of a two-hundred dollar fine or two months in jail. Since fines were an enormous burden, the students chose jail. They were immediately transferred from the city jail to Parchman State Penitentiary. There, nine black girls were locked in one filthy cell with the white girls occupying an adjoining cell. The cells contained nothing but mattresses and sheets thrown on the steel floor. When the girls began to sing freedom songs, prison guards took their mattresses away. When they sang the Star-Spangled Banner the guards took their sheets away. For three nights they slept on the steel floor.

The male prisoners also sang freedom songs and their mattresses and sheets were also taken away. The men were beaten, and two of them had "wrist-breakers" applied to their arms, devices by which a prisoner can be spun around and around until his arm is broken.

One of the two so treated was a Howard University philosophy student named Stokely Carmichael. Carmichael had been a senior in New York City's top-graded Bronx High School of Science when the four Greensboro freshmen began the first sit-in. He went on to Howard and joined the Howard chapter of SNCC which called itself the Nonviolent Action Group and was cheerfully known as NAG. (Nag the segregationists enough and they may give in.)

The separately titled Howard chapter was indicative of the free-wheeling lack of central organizational control in those early days of SNCC. Like the sit-ins which had given rise to it,

SNCC grew and spread by a kind of spontaneous combustion. Each college chapter seemed self-propelled. Its members were apt to launch projects without going through channels to get permission—as CORE, SCLC, and Martin Luther King were about to discover.

That June, Dr. King and the SCLC reluctantly agreed to a government appeal to postpone Freedom Rides temporarily to avoid further white mob violence. But black and white SNCC students in Atlanta, in Nashville, in Washington, and points north, often accompanied by their college professors and chaplains, went on boarding buses and Freedom Riding through the South. From June through August they kept coming, organizing their own Freedom Rides as they had organized their sit-ins, continuing to arrive in Mississippi to be beaten and jailed for trying to enforce the desegregation of bus terminals.

The Voter Registration Drive

But by August 1961, SNCC was becoming increasingly involved in a new and more far-reaching project. Earlier, Tim Jenkins, Negro Vice President of the National Student Association, had come to SNCC with a proposal made to him by representatives of the Taconic and the Marshall Field Foundations with the support of Burke Marshall, Assistant Attorney General. The foundations were offering to raise the necessary funds for a voter registration drive in the South—if SNCC would provide the manpower (and the courage). The plan was accepted by SNCC largely due to a remarkable SNCC leader named Robert Parris Moses.

Born in Harlem, educated at Hamilton College and with a master's degree in philosophy from Harvard, Robert Moses had left a teaching job at Horace Mann, an old and distinguished private school for boys in New York, to work full time for SNCC, and in the summer of 1960 had travelled to Mississippi on a field trip. There, from Reverend E. W. Steptoe, Negro farmer and minister, and head of the NAACP in Amite County, Moses learned about voting in Mississippi. Negroes who wished to vote had to answer twenty-one questions and to interpret any section of the Mississippi Constitution which the white registrar might choose. The Mississippi Constitution has two hundred and eighty-five sections.

From Reverend Steptoe, Moses also learned that although Negroes constituted forty-three percent of the state's population, only five percent of them had ever been permitted to register. No Negro held even the smallest local public office. The median annual income for a Mississippi black family was $1100, earned by working for whites as household servants or tenant farmers—the only jobs open to blacks in Mississippi. White men also owned the land on which black families built their flimsy tar-paper shacks or one-room wooden houses. At the very least, a Negro who tried to register in Mississippi would risk his job, his income, and his home. He would risk having his house burnt to the ground and his churches bombed. If he persisted, he risked floggings by the Ku Klux Klan and death at the hands of any white man who owned a gun and chose to use it.

In the summer of 1961, Bob Moses and Robert Zellner, a white student from Alabama, arrived in McComb, a back-country town in Pike County on the Louisiana border. In nearby Amite County, in the Reverend Steptoe's farmhouse, they set up the first voter-registration school. Black men and women began attending classes to learn the intricate provisions of the Mississippi Constitution.

On August 15, Moses accompanied three pupils—two middle-aged women and an elderly farmer—to the Amite County Courthouse to fill out the necessary registration forms. Their sudden arrival at the registration office took the clerk so by surprise that he permitted the Negroes to fill out the forms without incident. But police officers, the sheriff, and a few white citizens were hanging around the courthouse. Their reaction was immediate: as Bob Moses returned to McComb, he was stopped and arrested by two men in a passing police car. ("Get in the car, nigger," said a cop to the Harvard master of philosophy.)

Two weeks later when Moses attempted to take four more black registrants to the courthouse, he was attacked on the street by Billy Jack Caston, a cousin of the local sheriff. Caston split Moses' head open with the butt end of a heavy knife and drove the would-be registrants from the courthouse steps at knifepoint. (The name of the town in which the Amite Courthouse stood was Liberty.)

Early in September, a SNCC worker in Walthall County accompanied his first two black voter-candidates to the county courthouse to register. A white official got a gun and ordered them out of the courthouse. As the SNCC student turned to leave, he was clubbed from behind with the gun butt. Bleeding and dazed, he stumbled out into the street, where he was arrested by the local sheriff on charges of "inciting to riot" and "resisting arrest."

As black residents continued to attend SNCC classes, the old Mississippi tactics of terror and intimidation increased. ("It's fear that keeps the niggers down," a Mississippi sheriff explained later to a Department of Justice investigator.) Negroes seen attending voter-registration classes were waylaid and beaten by whites on their way home. Some were threatened with death if they persisted in attending classes. One of these was a black farmer named Herbert Lee. He had been seen attending SNCC classes and had been ordered to stop. He continued to attend classes.

At noon, on September 25, 1961, as he sat in his delivery truck in front of the Liberty cotton gin, Lee was gunned to death in full view of three Negro farmers. According to the witnesses, E. H. Hurst, member of the Mississippi State Legislature and father-in-law of Billy Jack Caston, had approached Lee, said something to him, and then shot him.

For two hours, Lee's body lay on the dusty ground touched only by flies. Finally a coroner's wagon drove over from McComb and took it away, and the sheriff's office announced that Lee had died "accidentally." Word of the murder spread through town, however, and the local newspaper next day carried the story that Lee had been killed "while trying to attack E. H. Hurst." No mention was made of Lee's reputation as a respected and hard-working farmer, or of the nine children he left behind.

The murder of Herbert Lee frightened many black citizens into dropping out of SNCC classes. But the fear which kept her elders from voter-registration classes angered fifteen-year-old Brenda Travis. Brenda and five of her high-school classmates had already been expelled from school for taking part in a Woolworth sit-in. Now, one hundred and eighteen strong, Brenda and her black classmates staged a march through the business district, carrying signs protesting Herbert Lee's murder and appealing to black Mississippians to register and vote.

Followed by an angry mob of white hecklers, the children marched to city hall to present a petition for Negro voting rights. They were all placed under arrest, and stood in line silently waiting to be booked, accompanied by Bob Moses and Bob Zellner. Two white men, enraged that Zellner was not only white but a Southerner, broke from the mob and attacked him, one trying to choke him while the other tried to gouge out his eyes. Committed to nonviolence, Moses could only shield his friend's body with his own until the police chief rescued the two young men by arresting them for disturbing the peace. "Ought to leave you out there," he said as he booked them.

The high-school students were arraigned on a variety of charges. (One thirteen-year-old girl was charged with "attempted murder" for having stepped on a white woman's foot.) Those who had taken part in the Woolworth sit-in were singled out for special reprisals. Brenda Travis, told she had broken parole, was sentenced to a year in a state reformatory.

Her sentence drove a hundred of her fellow students to march silently to city hall the next day to appeal for mercy. They were arrested as they knelt praying on the city hall steps. When they were freed on parole, they were told by the Negro high-school principal that they would all be expelled unless they signed a pledge to refrain from all Civil Rights activities. They refused to sign the pledge, and in October young SNCC volunteers opened "Nonviolent High"—a high school for the expelled children.

Although sit-ins continued, the registration drive, financed by foundations and by contributions from such groups as the National Council of Churches, had now become SNCC's chief project. Many young SNCC workers were taking a one-year leave of absence from college to work in Mississippi at salaries ranging from ten to fifty dollars a week, money which often went for food for Negro families in which the breadwinner had been fired, jailed, or murdered for trying to register. The SNCC work force grew swiftly, and included not only black students from the South (by far the majority) and North, but white students too: Jane Stembridge of Virginia, SNCC's first paid Secretary, and Bob Zellner of Alabama were only two of the white Southerners who incurred an extra measure of hatred in Mississippi for championing the cause of the black man.

In November, Bob Moses and eleven other SNCC workers were imprisoned in the "drunk tank" of the Amite County Jail on a charge of "disturbing racial harmony." By then the beatings of SNCC workers and black would-be voters, the murders, threats of murder, and KKK floggings had reached such proportions that Martin Luther King, Jr. telephoned President Kennedy demanding that the federal government intervene in "the reign of terror in Mississippi."

But, as the Justice Department was to insist over and over in the next few years, the maintenance of "law and order" was a "state matter" and not subject to federal control. "Law and order" were to remain in the hands of Southern sheriffs and white segregationists who were free in effect to shoot black men at will, as they were free to maintain Mississippi's illegal segregation with fire hoses, police dogs, cattle prods, beatings and prison sentences.

Enter COFO

Moses and his SNCC co-workers were let out of jail in December, and shortly after the new year of 1962 began the group left McComb and pushed deeper into the Delta region to Jackson. There they would spend the rest of the winter laying the groundwork for a summer Mississippi registration drive that would blanket the state.

This drive now became the chief object of the country's major Civil Rights organizations: the NAACP, CORE, and SCLC joined forces with SNCC to create the Council of Freedom Organizations—COFO—thus providing the student-teachers of SNCC with legal aid from the NAACP, direct-action picket lines and marches organized by CORE, and the immense local influence and prestige of Dr. King's SCLC. With plans laid in the winter, and money on its way from the Taconic and Field Foundations, COFO was ready by spring to open Freedom Schools and voter-registration drives in such far-flung areas as Laurel and Hattiesburg in southeast Mississippi, Holly Springs in the center of the state, Greenville and Cleveland on the Arkansas-Mississippi border, and Ruleville and Greenwood in Leflore County north of Jackson.

Leflore County was typical of the extent to which Mississippi deprived its black citizens of their voting rights and used economic means to keep them down. The county's population was more than sixty percent Negro, but whites owned ninety percent of the land. Ninety-five percent of the white residents of Leflore were registered. Two percent of the Negroes were registered. When, in the summer of 1962, SNCC opened a voter-registration school in the town of Greenwood, a white mob attacked the office, forcing the young SNCC workers to escape down a back stairway. The office windows were smashed and equipment destroyed. Yet SNCC persisted, and an increasing number of black voters continued to turn up at the county courthouse to register. The registrar announced that only half a dozen had passed the test, but even half a dozen was too many for Leflore County. The county is a poor farm area and winters are hard, especially for the Negro tenant farmers who work inferior land. They depend on government surplus food stocks to get them through the winter. In October of 1962, Leflore County stopped distributing food to 22,000 desperately poor farmers.

In Marshall County, a sheriff kept careful note of all Negroes who attempted to register or who were seen attending SNCC or COFO classes. Negroes on the sheriff's list who worked at menial jobs for the city or county they lived in were fired. Negro farmers who applied for routine bank loans were turned down. The few farmers who owned their own small plot of land found their taxes suddenly doubled. Unable to get bank loans they were evicted and forced to move. One man was forced to house his wife and eleven children in a tar-paper shack that winter, without food or clothes or firewood.

As economic screws tightened throughout the state, the food shortage among destitute Negroes reached starvation proportions. Word went out from SNCC offices to colleges all over the country and a massive food and clothing drive began on campuses, North and South. That Christmas week, two SNCC volunteers drove a truckload of food, clothing, and vitamins the thousand miles from Michigan to the Delta—only to be stopped by Mississippi police, arrested on a charge of possessing narcotics (the vitamins and a few bottles of aspirin), and held in jail for eleven days. When they were released their entire load of food, clothing, and vitamins was confiscated. One of the two, Ivanhoe Donaldson, refused to quit. From then on he served as a one-man relief agency, making twelve

Ruleville, Mississippi, 1962: Mrs. Joseph MacDonald points to bullet holes in the door of her home. Her husband also lost his job for registering black people to vote. *National Guardian*

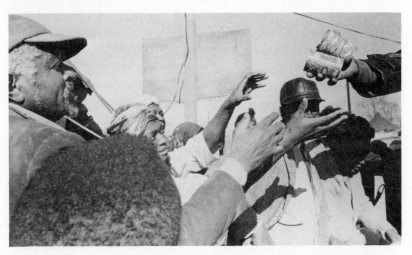

A SNCC volunteer hands out food to destitute black families in Mississippi. *Bob Fletcher, SNCC*

separate trips from Michigan to Mississippi to bring food and clothing to destitute families.

In other COFO centers, reprisals were physical, reaching a savagery easily equal to that of Nazi Germany. Seventeen-year-old college freshmen who committed the crime of teaching voter-registration classes were sent to Parchman State Penitentiary, where they were put in the "sweat box," a cell about six feet square without air holes or light. Said one boy: "As long as they don't turn the heat on, you can make it."

One group of teen-agers was kept in the sweat box for a total of thirteen days. When they were let out, some of them had suffered permanent damage to their eyes and lungs.

In Ruleville, Mrs. Fannie Lou Hamer, forty-seven and the mother of two children, went down to the courthouse to register in that winter of 1962-1963. The next day she was fired from the plantation where she had worked for eighteen years. Shortly after that, she was arrested and taken to the local jail. She was put in a cell where three white men, one of them a state trooper armed with a blackjack, and two Negro prisoners, waited for her.

"The state trooper gave one of the Negroes the blackjack," Mrs. Hamer later recounted, "and he said . . . 'I want you to make that bitch wish she was dead. . . .'" The prisoner beat her with the blackjack all over her body while the white men held her down.

For teaching Jackson Negroes their voting rights, one black college girl that winter was sentenced to two years in a reformatory. In Clarksdale, a local nineteen-year-old black girl who had attended COFO classes was arrested and taken to jail. There she was ordered to lie down on the floor, and was stripped and held down by prison guards while another guard beat her between the legs with a leather strap.

In May of 1963 the spotlight once more centered on Jackson. The state's NAACP field secretary, Medgar Evers, enlisted SNCC volunteers in his drive to desegregate the city of Jackson by means of the standard sit-ins and boycotts. Once more SNCC students were arrested and jailed for sitting in and for carrying picket signs. Once more, black students bore the brunt of white violence: black SNCC students were pulled out of peaceful marches and beaten by bands of whites while the police looked on. Once more, their elders rallied behind the young and boycotted the Jackson stores. So effective was the boycott that Medgar Evers was ready to force the mayor and Jackson's business leaders to open job opportunities as well as lunch counters to Negroes when, on the night of June 11, he was ambushed and shot to death outside his home. Witnesses identified the murderer as Byron dela Beckwith. Dela Beckwith was temporarily jailed, and was visited in jail by the Governor of Mississippi.

Ten hours after the murder, two hundred Negro teen-agers marched through the streets of Jackson carrying American flags and wearing NAACP T-shirts. On one of the T-shirts was a hand-lettered message: WHITE MAN, YOU MAY KILL THE BODY BUT NOT THE SOUL. (In the revolutionary Sixties the word *soul* was to become a kind of password of courage and brotherhood among the members of the new black generation.)

In Jackson, merchants now agreed to serve and hire Negroes. And on the day Medgar Evers was buried in Arlington National Cemetery, the Mayor of Jackson swore in the city's first black policeman.

Other Parts of the Forest

The obstacles encountered in the statewide registration drive in Mississippi did not deter SNCC from its promise to man voter-registration drives throughout the deep South. Back in 1961, a handful of SNCC students had arrived in southwest Georgia to open Freedom Schools.

The Georgia drive was centered in the city of Albany. There SNCC joined forces with the NAACP and the Baptist

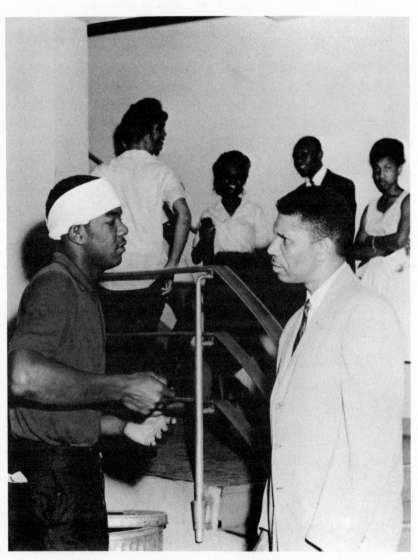

Mississippi NAACP leader Medgar Evers (right), only a few days before he was murdered by a sniper's bullet, listens to a youth beaten by police. *NAACP*

Ministerial Alliance to launch the Albany Movement, which combined a voter-registration drive with a nonviolent action drive to desegregate the city's illegally segregated public buses, bus terminal, parks, and library.

In December of 1961, eleven SNCC students were arrested for using the "white" waiting room in the Albany terminal. On the day of their trial, four hundred black Albany high-school students marched to the courthouse singing freedom songs. They were arrested and kept standing in the rain for two hours as the police booked them. Slater King, a Negro real estate agent and leader of the Albany Movement, was arrested when he led seventy black residents to the steps of the city hall where they knelt praying.

As the police chief afterward explained to reporters, "We can't tolerate the NAACP or the SNCC or any other nigger organization to take over this town with mass demonstrations."

The point was driven home by a deputy sheriff who took Slater King's wife into custody and—though she was five months pregnant—beat her unconscious. (The baby was later born dead.) King's brother was also beaten bloody by a sheriff hoping to stop the Albany Movement.

In February of 1963, in Selma, Alabama, thirty-two black schoolteachers were fired from their jobs for trying to register to vote. More than three hundred of Selma's black residents were arrested for attending voter-registration classes, passing out voter-registration leaflets, and otherwise encouraging the black people of Selma to line up at the courthouse on Registration Day, October 7.

When that day came, the line began forming early in the morning; SNCC director James Forman, accompanied by novelist James Baldwin, surveyed the results of the long voter-registration drive. By noon, more than three hundred and fifty black men and women were standing patiently in line waiting

Registering to vote in Americus, Georgia. *Liberator*

to register. Also surveying the line were a sheriff and two of his deputies and, at a little distance from them, two Justice Department officials and two FBI men.

Twelve Negroes were registered. Then the courthouse doors closed. All morning and all afternoon the black would-be voters stood patiently in line, and all morning and afternoon the doors remained closed. Three SNCC students stood near the line discussing the situation. The sheriff and his deputies walked past the federal men, seized the three students, loudly arrested them for "unlawful assembly," and hustled them off to jail— as the FBI and Justice Department men stood by with blank faces. (Local FBI agents stationed in the Deep South were almost invariably white Southerners.)

The afternoon wore to evening and still the courthouse doors did not open. A black lawyer turned to one of the FBI

Birmingham, Alabama, 1963: A black demonstrator is knocked off his feet as firemen turn on hoses during a protest march. *CORE*

men and asked whether he thought any violation of federal law was taking place.

"No comment," said the FBI man.

A SNCC student arrived with sandwiches and coffee for people on line who had stood eight or nine hours without food. A major in charge of an Alabama State Trooper detachment saw the SNCC student and shouted "Get 'im!" The troopers fell on the student, clubbed him to the ground, and jabbed him with cattle prods as the FBI and Justice Department men looked on.

The courthouse doors remained closed; night came, and Registration Day was over. Of three hundred and fifty black citizens, all constitutionally entitled to register and vote, twelve had been permitted to register.

Across the South, in the summer and fall of 1963, the Civil Rights revolution spread and white violence mounted. A thousand demonstrators were beaten and jailed by police in Greensboro, fourteen hundred in Durham, and another fourteen hundred in Orangeburg. In Cambridge, Maryland, black demonstrators were beaten and arrested by the hundreds and martial law was declared. In Danville, Virginia, a SNCC de-

Nashville, Tennessee, 1963: Police force young blacks away from the front door of a cafeteria they are picketing. *National Guardian*

segregation drive inspired sixty-five local students to march one night in a singing procession. Of the sixty-five, forty-seven were bloodied by police clubs and gun butts.

That was the summer in which 200,000 black and white Americans joined the famous March on Washington to petition the American conscience for black America's rights, massing at the Lincoln Memorial to hear Dr. King proclaim:

"I have a dream!"

His dream of freedom and brotherhood was answered less than a month later in Birmingham: four little girls sitting in a Sunday School class in a Negro church were killed by a bomb tossed into the church by white men. Two months after their death, President Kennedy himself was cut down by shotgun blasts as he rode in a motorcade through the streets of Dallas. The country was, in fact, embarking on an era of violence and murder which was to spread from coast to coast with unprecedented ferocity.

Yet if, as many liberals believed, John Kennedy had died a martyr to the cause of Civil Rights, his death brought that cause a victory he had been unable to achieve in life. The new President, Lyndon B. Johnson, was a white Southerner, and as such was able to obtain passage of Kennedy's Civil Rights Bill by winning a measure of Southern acceptance of it.

One of the provisions of the new law at last gave the federal government the right to intervene in Mississippi murders, by regarding them not as murders but as denials of Civil Rights. Late in 1963 Louis Allen, one of the black McComb residents who had witnessed Herbert Lee's murder, was warned by the McComb sheriff not to go to the Justice Department with his story. The sheriff underlined the warning by breaking Louis Allen's jaw with a flashlight. In January, word spread that Allen intended to leave Mississippi for Washington to tell his story. He was shot to death one night as he stood on the porch of his home. The incident was a prelude of the Mississippi bloodbath to come in the summer of 1964.

Mississippi Freedom Summer

In the spring of 1964, COFO announced plans for a state-wide Negro registration drive throughout Mississippi, to be known as the Mississippi Freedom Summer or the Mississippi Summer Project. That spring, under the auspices of the National Council of Churches, more than seven hundred SNCC students, NAACP lawyers, college professors, and ministers met to attend the first orientation classes for volunteers about to go into Mississippi for the first time. The volunteers were trained in nonviolent techniques: how to withstand beatings without fighting back; how to accept the kicks and curses of hecklers without fighting back; how to protect oneself against Mississippi's prisons, cattle prods, police, sheriffs, and mobs.

Volunteers who were considered unable to withstand the ordeal of Mississippi were sent to other less dangerous states to help in Negro registration drives. (One SNCC volunteer, a white girl from Colby College in Maine, was unable to get her parents' permission to go into Mississippi. She was instead sent by COFO to Brewster, Maryland, where "all the cops carried big black rawhide whips and wore high riding boots, and the combination made us think of Nazi storm troopers. Nazis with a Southern accent.") But the main COFO drive was the Mississippi Summer Project, and as the summer of 1964 wore on, the Project dominated the nation's headlines.

One of the SNCC volunteers was a twenty-one-year-old white college girl from New York City. Call her Mary. (Asked by the author whether she would be willing to have her name used, "Mary," who is now a housewife in New York, said, "Oh, no! I would never let my parents know what went on down there; they'd never get over it if they found out.")

Mary's assignment was to teach a class in the Constitution in a COFO school in Jackson, Mississippi. She lived with a black family in their wooden house on a dirt road on the out-skirts of town. The father of the family was a chauffeur who had to support a wife and six children on fifty dollars a week. They lived in a three-room house, the main room serving as kitchen-and-living-room, the other two rooms bedrooms containing one bed each. The father and mother slept in one bedroom; the six children shared a single bed in the other bedroom. That summer, the children shared their bed with Mary.

"We never saw meat. The mother would put a big pot of beans and collard greens on the back of the stove in the morning and it simmered there all day. Each of us took as much as we thought was our share. We were always hungry."

Mary wanted to pay for her room and board, but "badly as they needed the money they wouldn't take a penny from me. They were shocked at the suggestion. They knew I was down there to help them. All the black families around Jackson took in SNCC kids. None of them would let us pay for anything."

One SNCC student teaching in Jackson was a black Harvard student who had been arrested repeatedly for teaching in Freedom Schools.

"His back was like a jigsaw puzzle of scars," said Mary. "They'd beaten him with clubs, whips, iron pipes. He wouldn't tell me what else they did. They used to torture them in prison in ways that wouldn't show when they got outside."

As to the SNCC girls, especially black girls, "nobody would believe what happened to them. Some of them were just kids, sixteen or seventeen. They'd help some local black people to register, and the police would arrest them and take them to jail for what the cops called an 'internal examination.' The examination turned out to be mass rape—by the sheriff, the prison guards, the prisoners. Three or four girls would be let out of prison after a few days and nights of steady rape, in such a state of shock they weren't sane anymore. They'd be rushed to hospitals or back to their families but a lot of them never recovered."

And there were the minor incidents.

"I was walking along the street one day in a nice white

residential section of Jackson," said Mary, "when a cop walked over to me and said: 'I know you, you're that nigger-lovin' Communist Jew bastard from New York—and hit me across the face with the flat of his hand and kept on hitting me till everything swam in front of me and I started to fall, and he jerked me back to my feet. When I could see again, I saw white people on the street, just passersby standing and staring at us. They seemed stunned by what the cop was doing but they were too uptight to interfere."

It was in the face of such terrorism that SNCC helped black voters to found a new political party in Mississippi.

Mississippi was a one-party state in which victory in the Democratic Primary was tantamount to election. And since Negroes were excluded from the party's caucuses and conventions, no slate of candidates ever included a single Negro. In the summer of 1964, with the help of such gallant local black leaders as Mrs. Fannie Lou Hamer, SNCC founded the Mississippi Freedom Democratic Party, which held its own party convention, ran its own primary, and allowed Mississippi voters to elect an integrated slate of delegates to the coming Democratic National Convention in August. Mrs. Hamer was one of the elected delegates. Few delegates ever paid so high a price for the simple privilege of registering to vote, and running for a delegate's seat. Mrs. Hamer and her husband had both been fired and were being starved by the white community, which not only saw to it that they could not get work but excluded the family from relief and welfare rolls—which, like "law and order," are "state matters."

No one ever counted the beatings, rapes, and attempted murders of SNCC students and Mississippi Negroes by white Mississippi that summer. No one counted the Negro homes bombed, the houses burnt down, the fathers fired, the families evicted. But someone did count thirty-three Negro churches burnt to the ground in Mississippi. And it was to investigate

The 1964 Mississippi Freedom Democratic Convention. *National Guardian*

one such church-burning that three SNCC students set out one night in their station wagon from the town of Philadelphia, Mississippi. The three young men—James Chaney, Andrew Goodman, and Michael Schwerner—were never seen alive again.

They were hardly the first men to disappear in the swamps of Mississippi. Murders of Negroes were so common in Mississippi as not to be considered newsworthy. But this time it was different: two of the three missing students were white, the sons of affluent Northern families. And the fact that well-to-do *white* students had disappeared in Mississippi made headlines throughout the country.

The press demanded an FBI investigation of the disappearance. After much prodding, the FBI arrived to search the swamps and bayous of Mississippi for the missing students. While the search went on, the television networks gave the story wide publicity, interviewing Mrs. Hamer of the Freedom Democratic Party, SNCC and COFO leaders, and Governor Johnson of Mississippi.

Mrs. Hamer told the story of her attempt to register and what it had cost her; SNCC and COFO leaders told of the terror, the beatings, the burnings, the bombings in Mississippi. Governor Johnson stated his case:

'The hard core of this group [COFO] is your beatnik-type people . . . they don't realize they're following a group of professional agitators. . . . We're not going to tolerate any group from the outside of Mississippi or from the inside of Mississippi to take the law into their own hands. We're going to see that the law is maintained, and maintained Mississippi style."

As the FBI search continued, the searchers dredged up from the rivers and swamps not the three bodies they sought, but the bodies of three other murder victims, all Negroes, one of them a teen-aged college student. Their murders had never been reported or investigated.

Andrew Goodman, 20

James Chaney, 21

Michael Schwerner, 24. *UPI*

At a SNCC training session for volunteers about to go down to Mississippi, new recruits and veteran instructors waited tensely for the news. The three missing students were their friends; Rita Schwerner, wife of one of the missing men, was there listening as Bob Moses spoke of six black SNCC workers murdered in Mississippi since December.

John Doar of the Justice Department also attended the meeting. He told the SNCC volunteers that the federal government could not protect them in Mississippi.

"How is it," asked a SNCC volunteer, "that the government can protect the Vietnamese from the Viet Cong, and the same government will not accept the moral responsibility for protecting the people of Mississippi?"

"Maintaining law and order is a state responsibility," said Doar.

"But how is it that the government can accept this responsibility in Vietnam?" asked the student.

"I would rather confine myself to Mississippi," said Doar.

Staughton Lynd, a Yale history professor who was directing the entire Freedom School operation, rose to point out to Doar that the federal government did have a legal right to send troops into any state in a time of crisis, and had often done so. In such a crisis of violence and murder as the present one in Mississippi, how could the federal government decline to interfere and still regard itself as a moral instrument?

Said Doar, "I just try to do the best I can under law. . . . I have no trouble living with myself."

It was Bob Moses who got the news when it came, and made the announcement: "The kids are dead."

The FBI had exhumed with a bulldozer the bodies of Chaney, Goodman, and Schwerner.

According to William Bradford Huie's full-dress account of the triple murder *(Three Lives for Mississippi),* the three young men had been arrested on a speeding charge, held briefly, and released. They returned to their station wagon and drove on, unaware they were being followed by carloads of armed white men, who easily overtook them. The white men forced the three students out of the station wagon, lined them up, and shot them through the heart. They piled the bodies into the station wagon and drove a few miles to a ditch. They widened the ditch to a trench with a bulldozer, threw the three bodies into the swampy grave, and covered them with two feet of dirt, trusting the rains and ditch mud to sink the bodies deep in a few months' time. The murderers then set fire to the station wagon and drove home to Philadelphia. (*Philadelphia* means "brotherly love.") There they were met by a Mississippi official who told them, "Mississippi can be proud of you. You've let these agitatin' outsiders know where this state stands. Go home now and forget it."

(Fifteen men were later tried for the crime; eight were acquitted, seven received prison sentences.)

By the end of the Summer Project, Negro voter-registration had doubled in Mississippi—from 25,000 to 50,000—and the delegates elected on the new Freedom Democratic Party slate had the promise of influential Democratic leaders that they would be seated at the convention.

The promise was not kept. The dreary deals of a political convention prevailed to seat the Mississippi segregationist delegation. Walter Reuther, Hubert Humphrey, and conservative Negro leader Bayard Rustin begged the Freedom Party delegation to accept a token offer of two seats. The offer was rejected.

"It was not enough for all the work, all the fear, and all the lives that had been lost," said Mrs. Hamer.

Yet they had won a historic victory for the future. Four years later, the Mississippi Freedom Democratic Party was to be seated by the Democratic National Convention, which at the same time outlawed the seating of any future delegation elected on a basis of racial exclusion.

Bitter Disillusionment

In the spring of 1965, while Dr. King was renewing the de-segregation drive in Selma, Alabama, SNCC launched another new political party next door in Lowndes County, Alabama. Lowndes County was eighty percent Negro; yet in March of 1965 there was not a single registered black voter on its rolls. Headed by Stokely Carmichael, SNCC volunteers moved into Lowndes to try to persuade black residents to register.

"But these people," wrote Carmichael in *The New Republic* in 1966, "said they didn't want to . . . enter a machine headed by George Wallace. To them, politics meant Wallace, Sheriff Jim Clark, and . . . a crew of racist bullies and killers. Entering politics meant . . . confronting the tools of Wallace: the county registrars who had flunked Negroes consistently for years.

"They asked if something different could not be created. . . ." And so in March of 1965, SNCC helped the black people of Lowndes to found a new party. Since Alabama law required political parties to have emblems, Carmichael chose "the big, bold, bad, beautiful black panther."

Which is how it happened that Mrs. Viola Liuzzo, a young white housewife who was driving marchers home from Dr. King's Selma-to-Montgomery March, had a sticker on her car reading "Pull down the lever for the Black Panther" when, as she sat at the wheel of her car, she was shot and killed by a white sniper.

In August, it was the Reverend Jonathan Daniels, a Negro minister, who was shot and killed on the streets of Haynesville, Georgia. In January, 1966, it was a twenty-year-old student named Samuel Younge, a SNCC volunteer in the "model" town of Tuskegee, Alabama, who was shot and killed by a white gas-station attendant for attempting to use a "whites only" washroom.

By this time, the contrast between the U.S. government's zeal to protect the lives and freedom of the citizens of South

Vietnam, while failing to protect the lives and freedom of black citizens in its own country, was too much for SNCC. In January of 1966, SNCC published a manifesto condemning American involvement in the war in Vietnam. It was the first of the Civil Rights groups to publish such a statement. Once more it was roundly condemned by the press for being "unpatriotic" and Communist-controlled.

In May of 1966, SNCC was invited to attend a White House conference on Civil Rights, and one hundred and thirty SNCC delegates met to consider the invitation. The students, black and white, male and female, Northern- and Southern-born, had much in common. All of them had been jailed in Southern prisons. Almost all of them, including the girls, had been beaten. Some had been tortured. Some had lost their health. (James Forman had a bleeding ulcer and a heart ailment.) All of them had seen young friends murdered. ("I've been to sixteen funerals since 1961," Stokely Carmichael told Jack Newfield.) Now they were being asked to attend another Civil Rights conference, to listen to more talk. SNCC workers remembered how much inspiring talk there had been three years earlier at that famous March on Washington. And what had been the result of it? In the three years since the March, not one act from the white power structure had backed up all the fine words. Not one positive change had been instigated by the government. The Civil Rights Bill was still mere words on paper to most of white America.

So, at least, was the view of Stokely Carmichael and those who sided with him that day, in a stormy internal battle for control of SNCC, with the white-liberal and King-oriented moderates on one side, and a new, militant group headed by Carmichael on the other. The Carmichael faction won the battle, and it was not long before Carmichael would announce the new direction SNCC was to take. The new SNCC was to seek not white support, white favors or white sufferance, but black economic and political power. The doctrine was first publicized a month after the SNCC conference, as a result of the attempt made on the life of James Meredith.

Four years earlier, Meredith had needed federal marshals and the National Guard to force a way for him into the University of Mississippi, where he became the first black student. Now he believed that things had changed. He believed that the conscience of Mississippi had finally been awakened. He set out to prove it. He announced that he would walk alone and unarmed through Mississippi, to prove that the day had come when a man might safely walk through his native state even though his skin was black. In June of 1966, Meredith set out on a two-week walk through the state. He was cut down by shotgun blasts on the first day.

He was rushed to a hospital where he was met by leaders of every Civil Rights group in the country. Once more, he and they were inundated with words of sympathy and outrage from the white establishment. On the following day, Stokely Carmichael addressed an angry rally.

"We been saying freedom for six years and we ain't got nothing!" Carmichael shouted. "What we gonna start saying now is black power!"

The phrase was not a new one, and the black audience to whom Carmichael spoke knew what he meant by it. But this time there were newsmen on the scene. The press picked up the phrase "black power" and gave it almost the proportions of scare headlines. The impression created was that Carmichael and the members of SNCC—who never had been known, separately or collectively, to carry a gun, assault anybody, burn, bomb, or murder anybody—were now about to rise up and make war on the white world. So great was the furore that Carmichael had to spell out what he meant, in an article published by the *New York Review of Books* in September of 1966.

Black Americans, Carmichael wrote, have two problems: "They are poor and they are black. . . . Almost from its beginning SNCC sought to address itself to both conditions with

The leaders of the three large civil rights groups march arm-in-arm in Canton, Mississippi. (left to right) Martin Luther King, Jr.; Floyd McKissick; Stokely Carmichael. *UPI*

a program aimed at winning political power for impoverished Southern blacks. . . . We had to work for power because this country does not function by morality, love, and nonviolence, but by power. . . .

"In Lowndes County, black power will mean that if a Negro is elected sheriff he can end police brutality. If a black man is elected tax assessor he can . . . channel funds for the building of better roads and schools serving black people." And in counties "where black men have a majority, they will attempt to use it to exercise control. . . ."

There was nothing revolutionary in all this. But behind it was a new militancy, born of bitterness.

"Each time the people . . . saw Martin Luther King get slapped they became angry," wrote Carmichael. "When they saw four little black girls bombed to death, they were angrier; and when nothing happened, they were steaming. . . .

"For too many years, black Americans marched and had their heads broken and got shot. . . . We cannot be expected any longer to march and have our heads broken in order to say to whites, 'Come on, you're nice guys.' For you are not nice guys."

"*We affirm the philosophical or religious ideal of nonviolence,*" the SNCC founders had declared in 1960. "*Through nonviolence . . . love transcends hate . . . peace dominates war . . . justice . . . overthrows injustice.*"

Through six years of murder, torture, beatings and imprisonment, the young of SNCC had remained steadfast to their commitment to nonviolence. But in 1966 the facts had to be faced: in Mississippi, in Albany, in Selma, love had not transcended hate; peace had not dominated war; justice had not overthrown injustice. And throughout the country, only a handful of white Americans cared. White America's attitude toward black America had not really changed. These were the facts that drove SNCC's young leaders, embittered by what Jack Newfield termed "unredemptive suffering," eventually to remove the word *nonviolent* from the organization's title. The new, more militant SNCC also discouraged white participation. Even before the Watts-Newark-Detroit ghetto uprisings, SNCC had found that too many well-meaning young white students were going to the South to point out the sins of white Southerners—while ignoring the sins of whites in their own Northern communities.

SNCC therefore now said to the white Northern students: Don't travel from Berkeley to Mississippi to end segregation in Mississippi; stay home and end it in Berkeley. Don't come from New York to demand an integrated education for Mississippi's children; stay home and demand an integrated education for Harlem's children. Justice for the black man—like charity—must begin at home.

This change in attitude on the part of SNCC reflected the change in the national Civil Rights movement, as its emphasis in 1967 switched from the oppressed black South to the oppressed black North. And it was at this juncture that SNCC's influence inevitably began to wane. Southern-based and Southern-oriented, SNCC had had its beginnings on the campuses of Negro colleges, in an area where such colleges were numerous. When the Civil Rights struggle moved north, SNCC had no such ready-made base from which to operate. There were few Negro colleges in the North, and few ghetto children could afford to enter white colleges; still fewer, educated in notoriously inferior ghetto schools, could pass the entrance exams. This situation was beginning to change in 1967; and the change would bring about another black student movement unallied with SNCC. (See Chapter IV.)

But if SNCC's high hopes ended in embittered disillusionment, its six years of heroic effort and undeserved suffering had not been in vain; SNCC students had in fact wrought some real and lasting changes in the grim lives of black Southerners.

For example, due entirely to one desegregation drive by SNCC in the city of Danville, Virginia, jobs were opened to Negroes for the first time in both local government and private industry; lunch counters, public parks, and public libraries were desegregated; token integration began at white primary schools, and the local trade schools admitted Negroes for the first time in the city's history; and a white and a black labor union merged to form one integrated labor union.

And this was only the result of one SNCC drive in one small city. SNCC had achieved similar gains in uncounted cities throughout the South. Often it worked with CORE or SCLC or the NAACP. More often it worked alone. As the organization which supplied the major share of COFO's manpower, SNCC could claim the major share of credit for doubling Negro voter registration in Mississippi and all of the credit for creating two new political parties, one in Mississippi, the other in Georgia. Nor was it the least of SNCC's achievement that the doctrine of black power as revived by Stokely Carmichael was to become accepted in the Sixties by white America as a legitimate demand of a young black generation for economic and political control in black communities, so long under the domination of the white power structure.

Idealistic and peaceable, courageous and long-suffering, the young crusaders of SNCC had wrought far more miracles than they realized.

2

THE ANTIWAR MOVEMENT vs.
THE MILITARY ESTABLISHMENT

Few plagues of the past were more dreaded than the disease known as yellow fever, which swept through great cities in the eighteenth and nineteenth centuries, killing whole families in a week, leaving thousands dead in a single epidemic. The victim knew he had the disease when his skin turned yellow. A few hours later he began to vomit thick black matter. The vomiting continued until the victim began to bleed blackish blood from every body opening and so died.

At the end of the nineteenth century, Major Walter Reed, a surgeon in the United States Army, risked his life again and again in a grim search for the cause of the disease. He traced it to the bite of a certain mosquito; men were then able to eradicate the mosquito by wiping out the swamps and cesspools in which it bred. For his heroic service in ridding mankind of yellow fever, the United States Army built a hospital to the memory of Walter Reed.

In 1964, the same United States Army offered this author $1000 to write a TV training film designed to teach American airmen to fly over enemy cities at night and release capsules containing 3,000,000 yellow fever germs, which would infect entire populations with the disease in a matter of minutes.

"Colonel," said the author to the man who offered the assignment, "I couldn't inject one child with yellow fever germs. Not for all the money on earth."

The Colonel looked surprised.

"You mustn't think of it that way," he said. "To me, it's just Project 217-A."

It was pointed out to him that the Nazis had given the same excuse at the Nuremburg war-crimes trials. They had arranged not to think of a crematorium as an oven in which children were gassed and roasted to death. To them, a crematorium was just "Project 217-A."

"If you don't write it, somebody else will," said the Colonel. And presumably somebody else did.

That was in June of 1964. Though the facts were not widely publicized, it was no secret that the U.S. Army and Navy were engaged in the production and stockpiling of huge quantities of poison gases and disease germs. But during 1965, a new word was to be added to the American vocabulary which would symbolize the nation's abandonment of moral and humane limitations on war weapons: *napalm*.

A product manufactured by the Dow Chemical Company, and technically a gas, napalm in use is a flaming jelly which, like an acid, eats human skin on contact, and can ignite whole villages, buildings and people together, into flaming torches. Thanks to the young activists of the Sixties, this particular poison gas was to receive unprecedented publicity, which would eventually turn the nation's attention to the whole range of inhuman weapons in the American arsenal. For napalm was one of the more inhuman weapons which, in 1965, the United States began to use in its war in the poverty-ridden Southeast Asian country of Vietnam. And that war was to be the second target of the young reformers of the Sixties.

The seeds of the war were planted back in the mid-Fifties when Vietnam won its independence from France. By international agreement, the small country had been arbitrarily divided, like Korea before it, into two separate countries: North Vietnam, which was Communist, and South Vietnam, which was pro-Western.

In 1961, President Diem of South Vietnam appealed to the United States for military aid in order to put down a rebellion in his country which was being led by the local Communist

Party, the Viet Cong. In sending the requested aid, arms and two detachments of air troops, President Kennedy believed he was honoring the SEATO (Southeast Asia Treaty Organization) agreement made during the Eisenhower administration. Under its terms, the United States was pledged to aid any member nation attacked by a foreign power. But South Vietnam was not under attack; it was threatened instead with civil war. Aid was nevertheless sent in the belief that if the pro-Western Diem government fell it would be replaced by a Communist government.

In the fall of 1963, a military junta deposed President Diem and murdered both Diem and his brother-in-law, Premier Nhu, an indication that the new regime was to be as repressive —and as unpopular—as the old. According to Tom Wicker *(JFK and LBJ)*, Henry Cabot Lodge, American ambassador to South Vietnam, flew home to Washington that November to tell President Kennedy that the junta could not survive unless the United States kept it in power by sending much larger shipments of arms and troops. It was for Kennedy to decide whether the United States was to intervene further in the internal affairs of South Vietnam. But on November 22, Kennedy was assassinated, and the decision fell to his successor. President Lyndon Johnson decided to prevent South Vietnam from going Communist at all costs.

Early in 1964, Johnson ordered more arms to South Vietnam, this time accompanied by American troops called "advisers to the South Vietnamese Army." In August of 1964, Congress passed the Tonkin Gulf Resolution, which gave the President the authority to take any action he deemed necessary to protect American troops anywhere in the world. This was not a legal declaration of war, but in August of 1964, United States troops were not involved in a war. They were merely intervening in a civil war in South Vietnam. And the United States had so often intervened in civil wars in South America without a declaration of war that the action was not new.

On February 7, 1965, however, United States planes in South Vietnam launched a bombing attack against North Vietnam. With that attack, the United States was actually at war with North Vietnam. Thousands of young Americans were now to be drafted to fight that war. The thousands would eventually grow to nearly a million.

The war was to be fought without the formal declaration of war by Congress which the Constitution required. It was to be fought not with conventional weapons alone but with new chemical weapons: napalm which destroys life and property, and defoliation chemicals which destroy the land. And it was to be fought in a country which had never threatened or attacked the United States and which was eight thousand miles away.

It was then that America discovered what was new about this particular war. What was new was the moral outrage of the young generation, which was expected to fight without questioning either the war's political necessity or its moral justification.

Out of the bombing attack on North Vietnam arose an anti-Vietnam War movement, which spread with such rapidity, springing up in so many widely scattered American cities at once, that no one seems to know when or where the first protest demonstration took place, or when or where the first young activist burned his draft card. But like every major reform movement of the Sixties, the antiwar movement seems to have begun on college campuses.

In March of 1965, within a month of the attack on North Vietnam, the new movement appeared at the University of Michigan, where faculty and students joined in a round-the-clock, day-and-night discussion of U.S. policy in Vietnam. The discussion, which included seminars, debates, and background lectures, was dubbed a "teach-in." That spring teach-ins were held in some fifty colleges, reaching from Berkeley in California to Harvard in Massachusetts. So far did they spread

Youth vs. the military establishment: "What was new was the moral
outrage. . . ." *Sheldon Ramsdell*

that the Britannica Yearbook dubbed 1965 "the year of the teach-in."

On many campuses, the teach-ins were organized by a new student organization founded in 1962, called the Students for a Democratic Society. (See Chapter IV.) SDS had devoted the first three years of its existence to Civil Rights projects, including the Mississippi Summer Project. In 1965 SDS organized students throughout the country in the first national protest march against the war in Vietnam. The march, which was held in Washington, D. C., in April of 1965, had 20,000 participants. The speakers who addressed them included Yale professor Staughton Lynd, who had directed the Mississippi Freedom Schools; political writer I. F. Stone, and Senator Ernest Gruening. The list of speakers, like the teach-ins, disclosed an alliance which has been too little noted.

In an era when so much has been made of "the generation gap," it is worth observing that the anti-Vietnam War movement saw the student generation backed up and led by distinguished members of the over-forty generation. Lynd, Stone, and Gruening were to be followed in the new movement by Dr. Benjamin Spock, poet Robert Lowell, novelist Norman Mailer, painter Ben Shahn, Yale chaplain William Sloane Coffin, Jr., and a host of prominent clergymen. These men were predominantly middle-aged, and they gave to the anti-Vietnam War movement intellectual weight and maturity. Yet from beginning to end, the establishment press was consistently to maintain that the movement was the work of what *Newsweek* called "a noisy minority" of students. The press was further to imply that this noisy minority was composed entirely of bearded, probably dope-taking, hippies.

Nevertheless, in 1965 the press accurately reflected American public opinion. When the teach-ins in March and the SDS march in April were climaxed in May by a nationally televised teach-in, much was made of the fact that 100,000 people participated from their living rooms. In a country of 180,000,000, the figure indicated that only a fraction of the American people opposed the war. A national poll that year disclosed that sixty-eight percent of the country approved of the bombing attack on North Vietnam. It was therefore against overwhelming public opinion that the young movers and shakers of the Sixties set out to challenge the country's formidable military establishment.

That spring, SDS took the lead in urging students who opposed the war to register as conscientious objectors when they appeared before their draft boards. If they were denied c.o. status, they were urged to become "draft-resisters." The government and the press would imply that all draft-resisters were "draft-evaders." But there was a fundamental and profound difference between the draft-resisters of the Sixties and the traditional draft-dodger simply concerned with saving his own skin.

Most of the draft-resisters of the Sixties were neither cowards afraid to fight, nor religious pacifists to whom fighting any war was a crime forbidden by the Ten Commandments. They were refusing to fight this particular war, in the belief that it was morally wrong and that the weapons being used by the United States were inhuman. Their position was basically the one their own country had established for the world to follow, twenty years earlier.

During the trial of war criminals at Nuremburg after World War II, it was the United States which insisted that a man must bear the responsibility for his own acts, even when he committed those acts on orders from his superiors. It was the United States which insisted that a man who tortured, or cremated, or shot to death, prisoners in concentration camps or helpless village populations, was guilty of the atrocities he committed even though he had been ordered to commit them by a commanding general or the head of his government. This

71

principle had been adopted by the Nuremburg judges. Known as the Nuremburg Ethic, it now came home to haunt the country which had formulated it.

The young protesters believed that the U.S. had no legitimate right to interfere in the internal affairs of South Vietnam or to make war on North Vietnam. They believed the war to be morally wrong and racist. News leaked out of "defoliation" chemicals which destroyed the land; of napalm; of bombing attacks on defenseless villages. Ordered by their government to commit such acts, many of the young men of the Sixties, holding themselves responsible for the acts they committed, refused.

Their refusal took three forms. Some sought and found legal means of avoiding the draft. A few avoided it extra-legally. Others resisted it illegally and went to prison rather than violate the dictates of their consciences.

Legally, students were exempt from the draft while they remained in college and made satisfactory grades. After graduation, they could avoid service in Vietnam by going on to graduate school and staying there till they reached the safe age of twenty-six. (The draft-age limit was twenty-five.) Those who could not afford graduate school could enter draft-exempt professions, notably teaching.

The extra-legal method was that chosen by most anti-Nazi Germans during World War II: exile. Young Americans who had joined the army or navy before the Vietnam War began, and who found themselves morally unable to fight that war, deserted their ships or their army units and fled to Sweden as political exiles. At home, young men about to be drafted fled to Canada. In choosing exile, these young men all sacrificed U.S. citizenship rather than fight in this particular war, a course the United States had applauded when Germans took it during the Hitler regime.

But perhaps the most courageous of the young draft-resisters were the heroes of the anti-Vietnam War movement:

those who declined to take refuge in a draft-exempt profession or a foreign country, and who chose to begin their adult lives in prison rather than fight in what they believed to be an immoral and inhuman war. These young men, when called before their draft boards for induction into the army, appeared and refused to serve, knowing that the penalty was prison.

Many signified their determination not to serve by publicly burning their draft cards. They and their supporters staged sit-ins in draft offices and picketed draft boards. In the spring and summer of 1965, draft-card burning spread to such proportions that in August Congress hastily passed a bill, signed into law by President Johnson, making it a criminal offense.

The bill did not pass unanimously. In the United States Senate, William Fulbright of Arkansas and Wayne Morse of Oregon were giving the young a powerful assist by becoming the country's leading "doves." (As those who favored the war were called first "war hawks" and then merely "hawks," those opposed to it became "doves" after the ancient Biblical "dove of peace.")

The issue was also becoming a major campaign issue in state and local elections. In Georgia, where he was running for the state legislature, SNCC charter member Julian Bond campaigned on an anti-Vietnam War platform. Elected by a wide majority, Bond was denied his seat by the legislature on the grounds that a man who actively opposed the war was a Communist. If the legislature's real objection to Bond lay not in the color of his politics but in the color of his skin, its attitude toward Vietnam War protesters was still shared by most of the country.

But that fall, more grim facts began to leak out. On October 31, 1965, U.S. planes bombed a friendly South Vietnamese village by mistake. On November 5, U.S. planes bombed a second friendly village by mistake. At the same time, newspapers and magazines published in England and in European capitals began to print news stories, photographs, and eyewitness reports from Vietnam, which were consistently omitted from American publications by self-imposed censorship. These stories and photographs were reprinted and widely distributed by American peace groups—photographs of babies whose faces were half eaten away by napalm, stories of whole villages set afire, the inhabitants turned into human torches as their skin and clothing were ignited by napalm flames. (Students burning their draft cards and sentenced to prison for it charged that the United States government did not consider it a crime to burn villages, or to burn men, women, and children alive, but did consider it a crime to burn a piece of paper.)

The moral outrage grew; the campus demonstrations spread. In October, 1965, *Newsweek* reported that 100,000 students had turned out "to march, teach-in, speak-out, sleep-in, in dozens of American cities." One week later the same magazine carried a story about a Vietnam Day demonstration organized by students at the Berkeley campus of the University of California, which attracted 14,000 marchers. Yet in the same issue *Newsweek* could still dismiss the entire antiwar movement as the work of "a noisy minority" of students who "didn't want to fight for their country."

The Johnson administration took a similar attitude. Attorney General Katzenbach announced that month that the antiwar movement would be investigated. "There are some Communists involved in it," he said. "We may very well have some prosecutions."

He was buttressed by the President himself, who declared that "even well-meaning demonstrators can become victims of Communist exploitation."

But the old tactics of silencing dissent by branding it Communist and threatening it with investigation, which had so effectively silenced the young of the Fifties, had no effect whatever on the young of the Sixties. With the imposition of stiffer prison sentences for draft-card burners, the card burnings not only increased but began to take on a religious character. In

"An act with consequences. . . ." Burning draft cards. *Duane Hall, RAT*

New York City's Union Square that November, five young men burned their draft cards in the presence of 1500 silent supporters, in a solemn ceremony which, said the Catholic magazine *Commonweal,* had "a quality so frequently missing from the sacred acts of the Church. Here was an act with consequences . . . a commitment backed by the willingness to risk five years of personal freedom." The ceremony opened with the reading of a poem and closed with the singing of "We Shall Overcome." One of the five draft-card burners was a thirty-one-year-old father. He burned his card, with its draft-exempt classification, because his conscience wouldn't let him remain silent and safe.

As the protests mounted, the establishment's reprisals increased. In Boston that fall, a draft-card burner was sentenced to four years' imprisonment, the longest sentence yet passed upon a youthful card burner. In El Paso, Texas, a young Army lieutenant who had marched in an antiwar demonstration was court-martialed and sentenced to a year in prison. Paroled after court litigation, he was warned by the army that his parole would be revoked if he spoke out against the war, the army, or the president.

In Durham, New Hampshire, six SNCC students were arrested for demonstrating against the war; in Albuquerque, New Mexico, fourteen students were arrested on the same charge. In Williamstown, Massachusetts, the superintendent of public schools announced that he would not recommend tenure for a history teacher who had criticized the war. In Los Angeles, in Des Moines, Iowa, and in Prince George County, Virginia, children were suspended from school for wearing badges proclaiming their opposition to the war.

But it was at Ann Arbor, Michigan, where the movement had first appeared, that government reprisals took a new turn. Fifteen college students arrested for sitting in at the local draft-board offices were immediately reclassified 1-A, told that they were no longer exempt by reason of their studies, and informed that they would be drafted and sent to Vietnam immediately. The Michigan Selective Service director announced that he regarded this as proper punishment for war protesters. General Lewis B. Hershey, director of the National Selective Service program, backed him up with a statement recommending that all students who opposed the war be drafted and shipped to Vietnam forthwith. This drew outraged objections from liberal Congressmen and lawyers, but did not anger the country at large sufficiently for the administration to disavow it.

If Hershey did not shock the country, the steadily rising Vietnam casualty list did. Weekly death tolls climbed into the hundreds, weekly lists of wounded into the thousands. By 1966, the death lists and the ever-rising monthly draft calls were beginning to have their effect on public opinion. So was another immense new influence: the family television set.

The Vietnam War had become the first war in history to be seen by millions sitting at home in their living rooms. Here was no movie or written descriptions; here was the war itself to be stared at. And despite the censorship imposed on newsmen and photographers at the front, the death and destruction of a helpless, poverty-ridden people thousands of miles from the United States had its grim impact on the viewer.

It was not alone the spectacle of an American general triumphantly waving an arm toward the ashes of what had once been a village, and saying happily:

"But we won it!"

It was the sight of makeshift hospitals, of children with arms and legs blown off, or babies crying beside dead parents. It was the realization that these were people who had never harmed the United States, and who were helpless victims of a war which appeared to be far less important to them than to the giant nation which had moved in and taken over their country. Slowly American public opinion began to change. The youthful antiwar movement began to attract more and more support from citizens of all ages.

It came first from the churches. By the end of 1965 the

Catholic Peace Fellowship, the National Council of (Protestant) Churches, and the Union of American Hebrew Congregations had all petitioned the government to end the war. Early in 1966, the nonsectarian National Emergency Committee of Clergy Concerned About Vietnam was founded. In less than six months it had one hundred and fifty chapters.

In March of 1966, an antiwar march down Fifth Avenue in New York drew 25,000 participants. In May, SANE—the National Committee for a Sane Nuclear Policy—sponsored a Voters' March to Washington in which 15,000 people carried the signatures of 73,000 voters pledged to support only those Congressional candidates who opposed the war. That spring, more than thirty Congressional candidates ran as "doves."

In Redwood, California, church and community leaders joined students in trying to prevent the Port Commission from subletting public land to the United Technology Center for the building of a plant to manufacture napalm for use in Vietnam. The Port Commission ignored the demands and the napalm plant was built. But the incident received nationwide publicity and added fresh impetus to the movement.

As the draft quotas grew, the vicious inequities of the Selective Service system came under increasing attack. During World War II, every young man of draft age was given a number and each month's draft quota was filled by pulling numbers from a bowl, lottery fashion. But in the Vietnam War, the Selective Service system was indeed "selective." In exempting all college students from the draft, the Selective Service was in fact drafting mainly those young men who could not afford college or were intellectually unable to maintain good grades.

In May of 1966, Selective Service examinations were held on more than two hundred campuses across the country. College students and high-school seniors preparing for college took a three-hour exam, their grades to be passed on to their draft boards, so that those who passed could be excused from the draft. This examination turned the public spotlight on the system and on its underlying rationale. Said one Chicago student:

"When a nation has a policy that poor people without the background to do well in school should die, it's something to worry about."

Said an English professor in Atlanta:

"It puts a terrible strain on the teacher, knowing that if you give a boy a C minus or a D instead of a B, he might wind up in Vietnam."

But it was Congressman Adam Clayton Powell of Harlem who made the most cogent comment.

"These tests," said Powell, "are reminiscent of Hitler's twin system of eugenics and education: weed out the intellectually deprived or socially undesirable by conscripting them for cannon fodder."

Martin Luther King, Jr. saw the underlying racism just as clearly and condemned it with equal bitterness. For in the United States it was preponderantly the country's black sons who were unable to afford college. Many of them were unable to go even to free colleges, since on leaving high school they had to become family wage-earners in poverty-level households.

As the war progressed, black casualties were consistently higher than white, in proportion to their share of the population. And young black wage-earners, drafted and sent to Vietnam, left families behind to whom their wages had meant the difference between a decent family income and a bare subsistence. Theoretically, a young man was exempt from the draft if his earnings were essential to a family. But in practice, each local draft board had the authority to decide who was to be drafted and who was not. The results were becoming a national scandal.

In Southern states, where not a single Negro was permitted to sit on any draft board, white men classified every young Negro 1-A, regardless of his family's economic dependence on him. At the same time, a Western draft board declared a certain high-salaried young film star exempt from the draft because he was "the sole support of his mother."

The underlying racism of the system was underscored by the fact that the country on which the U.S. was waging the most inhuman of its wars was nonwhite. Civil Rights groups joined the antiwar movement in a body. As 1967 opened, Dr. King of SCLC, Floyd McKissick of CORE, and Stokely Carmichael of SNCC joined with the leaders of student groups, pacifist groups, and religious antiwar groups as cosponsors of a Spring Mobilization to End the War in Vietnam. On April 15, 1967, the Mobilization sponsored two massive protest demonstrations, one in New York, the other in San Francisco, which between them attracted more than 180,000 participants.

Shortly after the two demonstrations, Dr. King and Dr. Benjamin Spock, long a leader in SANE, announced the launching of the "Vietnam Summer," patterned after the Mississippi

April 16, 1967: (clockwise) Rev. James Bevel, Dave Dellinger, Dr. Benjamin Spock, Cleveland Robinson, Dr. Martin Luther King, Jr., and Mrs. Dagmar Wilson present a formal note protesting the Vietnam War to Dr. Ralph Bunche at U.N. Headquarters in New York. *United Nations*

Freedom Summer of 1964. Vietnam Summer employed 26,000 volunteers and 500 paid staff members to set up more than 700 antiwar projects throughout the country. The projects included teach-ins, sit-ins, and legal aid centers where young men could get legal advice on resisting the draft and legal counsel if arrested.

Meanwhile the Spring Mobilization leaders, under the chairmanship of Dave Dellinger, editor of *Liberation* magazine, were laying plans for a National Mobilization to take place in October. The National Mobilization to End the War in Vietnam was to embrace all antiwar groups throughout the country and all their unaffiliated supporters—anyone at all, in fact, willing to participate in a massive peaceful march to Washington similar to the 1963 Civil Rights march. The Mobilization would assemble at the Lincoln Memorial to hear speeches; the marchers would then cross the bridge into Virginia and march to the Pentagon, their object being to close the Pentagon for one day in symbolic protest against the war.

At a press conference held in August, the Mobilization Committee ran the gamut from Father Hayes of the Episcopal Peace Fellowship to Abbie Hoffman, leader of the new revolutionary Youth International Party, known as the "Yippies." Also present was William Pepper, executive director of a political coalition calling itself The National Conference for the New Politics. (If the organization was not destined to become a national byword, the last two words of its title were.)

On the day of the October march, the Pentagon prepared to welcome the peaceful protesters by ordering to the scene 1500 metropolitan police, 2500 National Guardsmen, 200 United States Marshals, and 6000 U.S. Army troops, with a standby alert issued to another 20,000 troops in the area.

On Saturday, October 21, 1967, between 70,000 and 90,000 people arrived in Washington. According to Norman Mailer, whose Pulitzer Prize-winning book, *The Armies of the Night,* is a full-dress account of the Pentagon march, more than a hundred antiwar groups participated. In addition to student,

October 21, 1967: Antiwar marchers assemble at the Lincoln Memorial in Washington, D.C. *Michael Hardy*

82

Civil Rights, pacifist, and religious groups, there were organizations of business and professional men, teachers' federations, political clubs, candidates, and elected officials.

A few hundred hippies and Yippies, who had clashed with police and so came without illusions, were armed with makeshift weapons. But the thousands upon thousands of others came as innocently as they had come for the Civil Rights march of 1963. The great throng assembled at the Lincoln Memorial and heard prayers and speeches. When the ceremonies ended, the marchers moved in small citizens' ranks, directed by monitors stationed along the way, across the bridge to the park and grounds of the Pentagon. They found facing them there long lines of military police armed with semiautomatic rifles, platoons of soldiers armed with guns and sheathed bayonets, and squads of police armed with guns and billy clubs. Reported the *National Guardian:*

"Unbelieving demonstrators just gaped at them, stunned, confronted for the first time by the guns of 'our boys.'"

To avoid violence, the demonstrators sat down on the grounds. Soldiers ordered them to move. Whether they refused, or whether in moving they were tripped by soldiers, the end was the same; marshals, police, and soldiers waded into the demonstrators, clubs and gun butts smashing the heads and faces of all they could reach. The *National Guardian* reported that the attackers' favorite targets were women.

One eyewitness account from Mailer's book will suffice. A Hunter College professor saw a soldier spill water on the ground where a young girl sat, in order to make it more uncomfortable for her. She cursed the soldier and shifted her body. Reports the professor:

"She lost her balance and her shoulder hit the rifle at the soldier's side. He raised the rifle and with its butt came down hard on the girl's leg. The girl tried to move back but was not fast enough to avoid the billy club of [another] soldier. . . . At least four times that soldier hit her with all his force, then as

83

The Pentagon march: "The soldiers ordered them to move. . . ." *Howie Epstein, LNS*

she lay covering her head with her arms, thrust his club sword-like between her hands into her face." Two more soldiers came up and began dragging the girl away. "She twisted her body so we could see her face. But there was no face there: all we saw were some raw skin and blood. . . . She vomited and that, too, was blood. Then they rushed her away."

Row after row of marchers advanced toward the Pentagon grounds to be met by armed platoons. A reporter for the Washington *Free Press* reported that while he was there, "One hundred people were methodically beaten and carried away to the paddy wagons." The attack on the marchers continued for thirty hours until, wrote the *Free Press,* "the resistance was broken and people, stunned at what they had seen and that they were still alive," left for home.

At the end of the day, an estimated six hundred people had been injured. The injured were American college students and their parents, teachers, and clergymen—attacked and beaten by U.S. Marshals, police, and the U.S. Army. The marchers had engaged in a peaceful protest; they had been answered with armed violence and bloodshed.

But in a democracy the military establishment is not supreme. It is under the control of the national government. The

Commander in Chief of this country's military forces is not a general but the President of the United States. The savage reprisals taken by the Pentagon therefore had ultimately to be laid at the door of the Commander in Chief.

It began to seem that the antiwar movement had all along been aiming at the wrong target. It had directed its civil disobedience and its mass protests at draft boards, induction centers, army installations, and finally at the national symbol of the military establishment, the Pentagon. But a decision to end the war in Vietnam could not be made at the Pentagon. It could only be made in the White House.

This realization had already given rise to the founding of the National Conference for the New Politics which had convened that summer in Chicago. The conference brought together left-wing political groups, Civil Rights groups, and disaffected local Democratic Party organizations, all of which hoped to form a coalition aimed at challenging the Johnson administration. (Since Republicans tended generally to be more "hawk" than "dove," opposition to Johnson and the war was far stronger in Democratic ranks and among splinter parties of the left than it was among Republicans and right-wing groups.)

The coalition itself failed, splintered by the conflicting aims of militant black groups on one side and middle-of-the-road liberal whites on the other, with the young "New Left," which was more Socialist than Democratic in philosophy, caught between them. But after the Pentagon march, it became obvious that the Vietnam War could be ended only by a frontal attack on the political establishment. As 1967 drew to an end, more and more people began demanding a "New Politics."

The phrase was to become the slogan for a new movement of the Sixties which began as 1968 opened, and which its leader was to dub "The Children's Crusade."

3

THE McCARTHY MOVEMENT vs.
THE POLITICAL ESTABLISHMENT

By the spring of 1967, the Vietnam War had become the country's overriding political issue. The war issue crossed the old party lines, so that for the moment the country's two political camps were not Republican and Democratic but "hawk" and "dove." In and out of Congress the cleavage between pro-war and antiwar factions became increasingly bitter. Nowhere was this attitude more evident than in the local and state organizations of the Democratic Party.

As President of the United States, Johnson was the head of his party. "Regular" politicians, who put party loyalty above issues, defended Johnson's escalation of the war chiefly on the principle of "my party, right or wrong—my party's president, right or wrong." Opposed to these were the Democratic "doves" in Congress and in local party organizations, who represented a growing number of antiwar—therefore anti-Johnson—rank-and-file Democrats.

As an incumbent president who had served only one full term, Johnson was presumed to be his party's automatic presidential nominee in 1968. This the Democratic "doves" refused to accept. During the spring and summer of 1967, antiwar Democrats split off from the regular party organizations to form insurgent Democratic groups.

With such names as "Dissident Democrats," "Dissenting Democrats," "Council of Concerned Democrats," and "Committee for a Democratic Alternative," these breakaway groups sprang up in California, Illinois, Iowa, Michigan, Minnesota, and New York. Their aim was to "Dump Johnson" at the 1968 Democratic National Convention. Their prime mover was a remarkable New Yorker named Allard Lowenstein.

In the coalition between the over-forty and under-thirty generations, Allard Lowenstein was unique. Having graduated from college in 1948, he was nearly twenty years removed from the college generation of 1967. But he had been president of the National Student Association in his youth, and over the years he had maintained so continuous a liaison with the student leaders who succeeded him that in 1967 he was still generally thought of as a leader of student politics. But Lowenstein had also served as an aide to Eleanor Roosevelt at the United Nations in the Fifties; through the Sixties he had been active in the New York Democratic Party's reform wing. Thus by 1967, though he had yet to be elected to public office, Lowenstein had been "in politics" for two decades, and it was said of him that he knew everybody.

Lowenstein had launched his Dump Johnson movement in the spring. In August he held a meeting of student leaders in order to involve college campuses in the movement. One of the student leaders asked him whom he had in mind to replace Johnson on the 1968 Democratic ticket.

"We'll build the base first," said Lowenstein. "The candidate will come along."

In September the student leaders returned to their campuses to help build the base Lowenstein needed. It was not easy. The college generation of the Sixties, including the activists, had an aversion to American politics. They distrusted both of the country's political parties with their rigged selection of candidates, their shabby back-room political deals, their cynicism, and the greed and graft constantly being exposed among the men they appointed to high places. Nor had the students' experience with Southern sheriffs, the Justice Department, the FBI, and the Selective Service system given them any great respect for the political system on either the local or national level. Nevertheless, their antipathy for the Vietnam War drove them to join the Dump Johnson movement and to agree to send campus delegates to a national Conference of Concerned Democrats which Lowenstein was planning to hold that winter in Chicago.

The Search for a Candidate

His base building, Lowenstein went shopping for a candidate. On the face of it, his search was preposterous: he was looking for a prominent Democrat willing to challenge the President of the United States for the presidential nomination of his own party. The influential men Lowenstein consulted told him he was insane. Lowenstein, an irrepressible, undiscourageable dynamo of a man, ignored them. He had a list of distinguished names of highly placed "doves"; one of them would just have to throw caution to the winds and agree to challenge the President for the presidency.

Accounts vary as to how many men Lowenstein eventually approached, but all accounts agree that he went first to Robert F. Kennedy.

In a national attitude unique in American political history and resembling the attitude of the British toward their royal family, the assassination of President John F. Kennedy had fixed the nation's attention on his younger brother, the Attorney General. A year later, when Robert Kennedy was elected Senator from New York, the expectation that he would one day follow his brother into the White House had reached the proportions of a national assumption. There were even jokes about it. When a Senate leader was accused of giving the younger Kennedy special consideration, he is said to have retorted, "I give him no more consideration than I would give any other future President of the United States."

This attitude—known as "the Kennedy mystique"—plus Kennedy's Cabinet experience, his "dove" status, and his position as senator from a large and politically important state, made Robert Kennedy the obvious man to challenge Lyndon Johnson. Accordingly, Lowenstein broached the subject to "Bobby."

But though Robert Kennedy wanted to be president in 1972, he did not mean to try for it in 1968. To oppose an incumbent president who was head of his own party seemed to Kennedy politically suicidal. It could only serve to split the party which he wanted united behind him in 1972. And if he lost to Johnson in Democratic primaries he would probably forfeit the party's nomination in 1972. He was only forty-one; he could afford to wait four years. Kennedy told Lowenstein he would not challenge Johnson in 1968. Later, when the press questioned him, Kennedy declared publicly that he would not run for president in 1968.

Lowenstein was now forced to look elsewhere. In *The Making of the President, 1968*, Theodore H. White states that he next approached General James Gavin and Senator George McGovern of South Dakota. Other writers have Lowenstein approaching Senators Fulbright of Arkansas, Morse of Oregon, Church of Idaho, and Hartke of Indiana. What matters is that somewhere along the line he approached Senator Eugene McCarthy of Minnesota.

On November 30, Senator McCarthy called a press conference and announced that he was a candidate for the presidency on the Democratic ticket, and that he would oppose President Johnson in a series of preferential state primaries in the spring of 1968. He explained to the reporters that he was "concerned" by the administration's plans for continued escalation of the war, and troubled by "the sense of political helplessness" felt by ordinary citizens who opposed the war. He hoped that his "challenge" would restore the faith of ordinary citizens "in the processes of American politics."

To millions of Americans watching the press conference on TV news broadcasts, Eugene McCarthy was completely unknown. He had had a long but relatively undistinguished career in Congress where no major bills bore his name. Millions of viewers seeing him for the first time saw a quiet, thoughtful man, a little remote, almost disinterested as he understated the extraordinary fact that he was about to challenge an incumbent president for his own party's nomination. He agreed with the reporters that he had little chance of defeating Johnson for the nomination, but he felt that his party and the voters needed an alternative to Johnson, and no one else had come forward. His calm, unemotional statements did not suggest the degree to which he was offering himself as a sacrificial lamb.

Eugene McCarthy had spent twenty years in Congress and in party politics. He was not innocent in the workings of political power and political revenge. He was openly opposing his own party's leader in the White House, which meant incurring the enmity of the regular Democratic organizations across the country. As the avowed anti-Vietnam War candidate, he was also incurring the enmity of the far more powerful "military-industrial complex." He was risking his Senate seat, his political future, and his reputation to enter a contest he knew he was almost certain to lose. It was an act of courage and self-sacrifice all the more impressive because in his quiet way he declined to call attention to it.

McCarthy's announcement of his candidacy was greeted as a joke by the press, politicians, the White House, and the country at large. The only group to take it seriously was Lowenstein's Conference of Concerned Democrats, which two days later, December 2, met in Chicago to hail its new presidential candidate. Some five hundred delegates from forty-two states attended the conference; and Theodore H. White's description of them remains the most accurate one yet written of what was to become known as the McCarthy movement.

The delegates, wrote White, were "overwhelmingly young, overwhelmingly clean-cut, overwhelmingly middle-class." He saw among them "few beards, fewer Negroes, no working-class types, and an extraordinarily large component of faculty and university types."

The atmosphere of the convention was electric as the delegates faced the size of their undertaking and the colossal odds against them. Their object was nothing less than to drive a President of the United States out of office. They were fired to a fever pitch of excitement by the shouting, table-pounding eloquence of Allard Lowenstein. (His fire-eating personality was to make Lowenstein anathema to the quiet Senator whose campaign he was launching, and would exclude him from the Senator's inner circle of advisers.) When Lowenstein presented their candidate to the delegates at the convention, Senator McCarthy made a brief speech, thoughtful, unemotional, faintly professorial. The delegates would probably have preferred a warmer, more passionate man, but it didn't really matter: Eugene McCarthy was not the creator of their movement, but only its finally emergent symbol. In a curious way, he was to remain its symbol rather than its leader. McCarthy would never control or direct the McCarthy movement; rather, he was to be borne along by it like a ship on a turbulent ocean.

Through December, the McCarthy candidacy made scarcely a ripple on the political waters, and the campaign seemed not to get off the ground. Of two hundred and forty-seven Democrats in the House of Representatives only one announced his support of McCarthy; none of McCarthy's fellow Senators did. President Johnson and Vice President Hubert Humphrey were jocular about the upstart candidacy, and the press took the similar view that McCarthy was a lightweight political novelty in this important election season.

But in the last week in January, the Viet Cong and the North Vietnamese launched the Tet Offensive, a massive assault on South Vietnam which nearly captured the seat of government, and made military claims that we were "winning the war" look ridiculous. American losses were staggering; more and more American sons were coming home in wooden boxes. When the Tet Offensive was followed by a request from General Westmoreland for 206,000 more Americans to be sent to fight in Vietnam, there was immediate public reaction. And public reaction now had somewhere to go.

In New York, the Committee for a Democratic Alternative —a statewide group of dissident Democratic "doves"—raised enough money to finance a full-page ad in *The New York Times* appealing to citizens to contribute money and time to the campaign of Eugene McCarthy. In the next week, similar full-page ads appeared in newspapers in sixteen cities across the country. By February, the antiwar groups were growing in force, and there was increasing interest in the impending Johnson-McCarthy contest.

The first of the statewide primaries was to take place in New Hampshire on March 12. In February, public-opinion polls estimated that McCarthy would capture fifteen percent of the vote, as against eighty-five percent for the President. The regular Democratic Party organization of New Hampshire—to which both New Hampshire's Governor King and Senator McIntyre belonged—was placing a large slate of Johnson delegates on the ballot. Governor King predicted that Johnson would "murder" McCarthy in New Hampshire. The press agreed. McCarthy was an unknown; he had no official party backing, no professional organization, no real financing.

But the governor and the pollsters failed to foresee what was about to happen. The young movers and shakers of the Sixties were about to take over Eugene McCarthy's campaign.

The Children's Crusade

Young McCarthy supporters had begun arriving in New Hampshire in January for weekends. The first contingents came from the nearest colleges: Amherst, Holyoke, Harvard, Smith, Yale. Groups of students left the campus on Friday afternoons and set out for New Hampshire on motor scooter, bike, bus, or two feet. Three hundred students from the Boston area hitchhiked. They brought their sleeping bags and their guitars, and set up the first McCarthy headquarters in Concord. With the Tet Offensive, fresh hundreds arrived from more distant campuses and set up more headquarters, sleeping in the headquarters and in church and synagogue basements lent them by sympathetic clergymen. When midterms ended in February, students arrived prepared to stay in New Hampshire until March 12, Primary Day.

They came from Columbia and Duke, from the University of Michigan and Berkeley, California, ready to cut classes for a few weeks, ready to give up political science lectures for something more real, something they were beginning to call "participatory democracy." They came with their peace buttons, their Beatle records and their way-out clothes, with their long hair and a few with their beards. They came with their A grades and their names on the Dean's List, proving as SNCC had proved, as SDS was about to prove, that the activists of their generation were those with the highest scholastic records. By the end of February there were five thousand of them in New Hampshire.

They arrived with no political experience, no campaign funds, and no professional direction. They set up McCarthy headquarters in fifteen New Hampshire cities, staffing and running them themselves. When the church basements were full, they slept on the living-room sofas and floors of local McCarthy supporters.

They decorated headquarters with signs reading GOD ISN'T DEAD BUT HE MIGHT COMMIT SUICIDE ON MARCH 12. IT'S UP TO YOU. They wore buttons with flower emblems and the word *Peace,* and buttons that said "We Try Harder" in Hebrew. They read that McCarthy was expected to get fifteen percent of the vote and they posted signs on headquarters walls to remind themselves what they had at stake in the size of McCarthy's vote:

Campaigning for McCarthy in New Hampshire. *Sheldon Ramsdell*

OVER 40%—WE GO ON TO WISCONSIN.
30%—WE GO BACK TO SCHOOL.
20%—WE BURN OUR DRAFT CARDS.
10%—WE LEAVE THE COUNTRY.

And they went out and campaigned for Eugene McCarthy as no candidate was ever campaigned for in the history of American politics.

They swept through the state ringing doorbells and they stopped every potential voter on the street. Bearded McCarthy students discovered that the conservative New Englanders distrusted young men with beards, and promptly shaved them off. New signs went up in McCarthy headquarters: GET CLEAN FOR GENE. The men shaved their beards and cut their hair, the girls let down their mini-skirts and declared a moratorium on eye makeup. (Boys unwilling to shave their beards banished themselves to back rooms and basements where they got out mailings and made phone calls out of sight of proper New Hampshire.)

They rang 60,000 doorbells and mailed 700,000 pieces of campaign literature. They enlisted the help of teen-aged street gangs to man sidewalk tables. They got high-school and grade-school youngsters to spend their Saturdays and the hours after school handing out McCarthy literature on street corners. Neat and clean, well-educated, well-dressed, the cream of America's affluent society and its finest colleges, they bridged the generation gap with their good looks and good manners and their passionate hatred of the Vietnam War, pulling more and more middle-aged New Hampshirites into headquarters, finding more and more New Hampshire homes open to them, eager to take them for a weekend or a week.

As the McCarthy student campaign mounted in strength, the establishment attacked them in predictable fashion. Senator McIntyre accused McCarthy of wishing to "honor draft-dodgers and deserters." Governor King said a McCarthy victory would "be greeted with cheers in Hanoi." Johnson radio ads blasted McCarthy and his students as "peace-at-any-price fuzzy thinkers who say 'give up—burn your draft card and surrender.'"

The weekend of March 8 through 10 saw so many last-minute student shock troops arriving from all over the country that frantic phone calls went out from New Hampshire to New York and California begging fresh train- and planeloads of students not to come. Twenty-five hundred volunteers were turned away from New Hampshire for sheer lack of space; every public and private shelter was packed to the rafters.

During that weekend before the Tuesday primary, on almost every major street corner in New Hampshire a young man stood with a placard round his neck reading: I AM A VIETNAM WAR VETERAN FOR McCARTHY. ASK ME WHY. All day long Saturday and Sunday, the young veterans stood answering questions, condemning the war, appealing to people to vote for Eugene McCarthy.

Celebrities arrived to lend their weight to the final push. A McCarthy rally in Manchester that Saturday night was graced by economist John Kenneth Galbraith, poet Robert Lowell, Hollywood stars Robert Ryan and Tony Randall, and superstar Paul Newman. The candidate himself, everywhere in evidence that final week, campaigned in a quiet, thoughtful, understated manner that was exactly right for conservative, laconic New Hampshire.

On Tuesday, March 2, 1968, Eugene McCarthy collected 42.2% of New Hampshire's Democratic vote, to President Johnson's 49.4%, in one of the most stunning upsets in modern political history. Because rival Johnson delegates competed with each other as well as with McCarthy delegates, McCarthy won twenty of New Hampshire's twenty-four delegates.

In delirious McCarthy headquarters, the victorious young were singing "On, Wisconsin!" and abandoning all thought of returning to college for the rest of the term. It was on that night that McCarthy himself dubbed them "The Children's

Crusade," in memory of the children's army which had set out for Jerusalem hoping to join the Crusades. These young people, too, were involved in a holy war.

The New Hampshire primary results stunned the country, and forced politicians and political commentators to reassess the national mood. Both groups believed that New Hampshire indicated not the popularity of Eugene McCarthy but the staggering *un*popularity of President Johnson. In political circles and in the press, the conviction was that McCarthy could never beat Lyndon Johnson at the Democratic National Convention—but that a better-known, more impressive candidate probably could. Once more, political attention focused on Robert F. Kennedy.

It was typical of the two men—and prophetic of the coming campaign between them—that on the night of March 12, when Eugene McCarthy was being cheered by a student army drawn predominantly from the most affluent homes and campuses in the country, Robert Kennedy was in California at the bedside of Cesar Chavez, organizer of a union of Mexican-American migrant farm workers and leader of their strike against the grape growers of California. Chavez was ending a twenty-five-day hunger strike undertaken to dramatize the plight of his people. Having lost thirty-five pounds, he had been too weak and emaciated to address a rally of his followers, and Kennedy had flown to California to speak to them in his place.

During the previous few weeks, as private polls had begun to indicate a far larger McCarthy vote in New Hampshire than had been dreamed of originally, pressure had been mounting on Kennedy to reconsider his decision not to challenge Johnson. Friends and supporters pointed out that McCarthy could never make it and Kennedy could. He had the magic name, the money to mount a massive campaign, and the backing of many political "pros" who would not back McCarthy.

A week before McCarthy's victory Kennedy had wanted to

announce his candidacy, but he was advised not to throw a monkey wrench into the New Hampshire contest. A day after the primary, the press asked Kennedy his plans. He said that he was "reassessing" his decision not to run. On March 16— four days after the McCarthy upset triumph—Kennedy announced that he, too, was a candidate for the Democratic presidential nomination. The timing added to the conviction throughout the country that Robert Kennedy had let McCarthy go alone and unsupported into battle against Johnson and now meant to reap the rewards of McCarthy's success.

By this time, McCarthy's Children's Crusade had moved on to Wisconsin to prepare for the April 2 primary. They set up headquarters in the rundown Wisconsin Hotel in Milwaukee, a few blocks from the plush Sheraton-Schroeder where McCarthy and his staff had their suite. They were busy organizing the thousands of new volunteers arriving from colleges in Illinois, Michigan, Minnesota, and Iowa, when they heard of Kennedy's announcement.

To the McCarthy students, Robert Kennedy was a coward who had lacked the courage to offer himself in November, and a calculating opportunist who had waited for McCarthy to prove Johnson could be beaten and now meant to steal McCarthy's victory.

But for the political "pros" in the McCarthy camp, there was now an agonizing choice. Both Allard Lowenstein and Richard Goodwin, former speech writer for President Kennedy, and now McCarthy's chief writer and adviser, were devoted to Robert Kennedy, who had been the first choice of both men as a candidate. Lowenstein remained loyal to McCarthy; Goodwin left to join the Kennedy staff. Two members of McCarthy's staff, Jonathan Schell and Jeremy Larner, were now asked to replace Goodwin as McCarthy's speech writers. Larner accepted the post; Schell left the campaign, unable to work against Kennedy.

If the McCarthy student army resented Robert Kennedy for

his entrance into the race, they reflected a national attitude which was to haunt the coming primary campaigns, and ultimately and permanently to haunt the country. For Robert Kennedy's announcement triggered in many segments of the population a hatred of him which would reach the proportions of a mania. Many explanations were offered by haters and nonhaters: he was ruthless, he was calculating, he was trading on his dead brother's name, he was an ex-Attorney General who had made powerful labor leaders and Southern segregationists his chief targets. Whatever the reason, the hatred of Robert Kennedy was to become as much a national assumption as his eventual arrival at the White House had been and would continue to be.

This dislike of Kennedy, coupled with the New Hampshire victory, caused a profound change in the attitude of the press and the public toward Eugene McCarthy. Where before he had been a joke, he was now a knight in shining armor, a hero fighting not one villain but two: Johnson and Kennedy. Long before the Wisconsin primary, the opinion polls and the press were predicting a major victory for McCarthy over Johnson there. (Kennedy had entered the race too late for his name to appear on the ballot.)

Wisconsin was to be McCarthy's largest numerical victory. But it was in Wisconsin that the proverbial "cloud no bigger than a man's hand" first appeared on the McCarthy horizon.

McCarthy vs. Kennedy

New Hampshire had been so stunning an upset that few people took note of the fact that the state itself was not typical. New Hampshire was almost entirely white and almost entirely middle-class. It had no great cities, no depressed, impoverished ghettos, no large minority groups. A few cities had one sizable quasi-minority group—lower-income French Canadian working-class people—and in the excitement of McCarthy's triumph few noticed that he did not carry those cities.

Wisconsin was more typical of the nation at large. Milwaukee had densely packed black ghettos. Eugene McCarthy did not campaign in them. Instead, reported Jeremy Larner, he "gave a speech on the race problem . . . to an audience of his young white followers." Shortly before Primary Day, McCarthy's press secretary, Sy Hirsch, and his aide, Mary Lou Oates, resigned from the McCarthy staff and left the campaign. They gave as their reason McCarthy's failure to speak out on the subject of Civil Rights. Questioned about this, McCarthy said that he knew the two aides had not been happy; he was sorry they had left; he hoped they would be back. On the substance of their grievance he said nothing. McCarthy's campaign issue was the war in Vietnam. He continued to address himself to that issue.

But on March 31—two days before the Wisconsin primary —President Johnson tossed the country its second political bombshell. Addressing the nation on radio and television he announced:

"I shall not seek, and I will not accept, the nomination of my party for another term as your president."

He topped this by declaring his intention to begin immediate negotiations with North Vietnam for peace talks.

Listening to this astounding broadcast, the McCarthy campaigners exploded with an excitement bordering on disbelief. The chief aim of their movement, which had sounded impossible a few months earlier, had suddenly been achieved: they had driven a President of the United States out of office. When, two days later, Wisconsin voters gave McCarthy fifty-seven percent of the vote, to thirty-five percent for the still-listed Johnson delegates, the victory was almost an anticlimax. The first and most momentous stage of the McCarthy movement had ended in complete triumph.

The second stage already looked outlandish. From now on,

the primaries would be fought not between the "hawk" Johnson and the "dove" McCarthy, but between two "doves"—McCarthy and Kennedy—at a moment when peace talks were already being planned.

Questions filled the political air. How soon would Johnson throw his weight to Vice President Hubert Humphrey as his own choice for the Democratic nomination? Would McCarthy

Appearing tired and in his shirtsleeves, President Johnson sits in the Cabinet Room of the White House, late March 30th, 1968, working on the address that shocked the nation. *UPI*

withdraw from the race in favor of Kennedy, to unite the anti-administration forces? And which of the three—Kennedy, Mc-Carthy, or Humphrey—was most likely to pull liberal Republican votes away from conservative Richard Nixon, the probable Republican candidate?

Influential pro-Kennedy Democrats appealed to McCarthy to withdraw from the race. But if McCarthy had seen himself as a symbol in November, he saw himself a successful vote-getter in April. He declared he had no intention of withdrawing in Kennedy's favor. (There had been bad blood between the two men since 1960, when McCarthy had backed Adlai Stevenson for the Democratic presidential nomination and Robert Kennedy had been the organizing genius credited with sweeping the convention for his brother John.) McCarthy pointed out that he couldn't throw his support to Kennedy even if he wanted to. Nor could he. McCarthy's support came from his Children's Crusade. Though his campaign was attracting more and more volunteer workers from the ranks of clergymen, suburban housewives, and college professors, his "children" were its base and its strength; and his children were nontransferable. They had made Eugene McCarthy their idol, the knight in whose service they meant to destroy the old corrupt political establishment, to build in its place a "New Politics." Most of them were to adhere to Eugene McCarthy with an unswerving devotion which Robert Kennedy was to regard with envy and respect to the end of his brief life.

McCarthy and Kennedy were to face each other in three primary contests in May—Indiana, Nebraska, and Oregon—with California and New York to follow in June. The first was the May 7 Indiana primary. A smaller, unpublicized primary was to be held in central Ohio on the same day. On April 3, the McCarthy campaign left Wisconsin for Indiana. Robert Kennedy was also heading for Indiana.

But American life does not stop for a presidential primary; certainly the ugly realities of America's race war do not stop.

On April 4, as he stood on the steps of a Negro motel in Memphis, Tennessee, Dr. Martin Luther King, Jr. was shot and killed by a white assassin. In the next twenty-four hours, riots broke out in the embittered black ghettos of more than a hundred American cities.

Kennedy learned the news as he landed at the Indianapolis airport. He was scheduled to speak at a rally in a poor black section of town, and he went directly there to break the tragic news to the crowd. The next day Kennedy flew to Cleveland to address the City Club and, abandoning his intended speech, delivered a moving eulogy of Dr. King.

McCarthy heeded the advice of the Secret Service men assigned to him to keep away from the ghettos, it wasn't safe to go there. He continued to deliver speeches against the Vietnam War and President Johnson.

As Kennedy barnstormed through half a dozen states, to make up for lost time, large crowds turned out, mostly out of curiosity. But as he rode down crowded city streets, standing in the front seat of his car, hatless, coatless, shirttails flying, hands reaching out to the people, the crowds who had come to stare were suddenly galvanized. They mobbed his car, tore off his tie and cuff links for souvenirs, reached out to touch him, shouted, "Hi, Bobby!" When he rode through the ghettos they shouted, "Soul brother!" and, "Make way for the President!" He seemed to derive strength from the mobs that hemmed him in.

When his car stopped, Kennedy made short impromptu speeches. He talked about the starving black child he had seen in a shack in Mississippi, about the teen-aged boy on an Indian reservation who had hanged himself in sheer hopeless despair. He talked about his Senate bills to bring new capital and industry into the ghettos.

McCarthy, campaigning in Indiana, talked about the war in Vietnam and Johnson's responsibility for it, as if Johnson were still a candidate and peace talks were not beginning in

Senator Eugene J. McCarthy and supporters in Indiana. *Sheldon Ramsdell*

Paris. A world-famous Negro leader had been murdered and riots were sweeping the ghettos, but no one listening to Eugene McCarthy or his youthful campaigners would have suspected it. (Said one New Yorker who switched from McCarthy to Kennedy that month: "McCarthy hides in the Vietnam War as if it were a cave.")

But as the Indiana and lesser Ohio campaigns continued, the real difficulty of the McCarthy campaign became clear. It was not a matter of racism, at least not among the McCarthy young. Somehow, McCarthy and his campaigners could relate and appeal only to people like themselves.

Reporting McCarthy's failure to win delegates in central Ohio, one of his campaigners, Professor Clayton Roberts of Ohio State University, pointed out that McCarthy carried the suburbs by a margin of two to one—and lost the overcrowded city of Columbus by two to one. The Indiana primary returns on the same day exposed even more sharply the exclusiveness of McCarthy's campaign. Indiana had been a three-way race. Along with McCarthy and Kennedy slates there were slates of delegates pledged to Governor Branigin, who was committed to the administration candidate, presumably Hubert Humphrey. Kennedy received forty-two percent of the vote, drawing his strength chiefly from the big cities, particularly the ghettos. Branigin won thirty-one percent, mostly from traditionally Democratic white working-class districts. McCarthy ran a poor third, his twenty-seven percent of the vote coming entirely from the well-to-do white suburbs.

The division in Ohio and Indiana established a clear image of the two anti-administration candidates. McCarthy spoke to and for a growing class of Americans: the well educated, middle- and upper-income whites, living in the suburbs. Kennedy spoke to and for the poor, the oppressed, the nonwhite.

In the Nebraska primary a week later, the results were particularly disastrous for McCarthy, since Nebraska's Democratic majority was made up largely of the poor, the black, and the

Despite a drenching rain, Senator Robert Kennedy campaigns in an open car in Omaha's north side black neighborhood. *UPI*

low-income white working class concentrated in Omaha and Lincoln. The result was that Kennedy not only carried every one of Omaha's fourteen districts but ran ahead of McCarthy in eighty-eight of the state's ninety-three counties, winning fifty-one and a half percent of the vote to thirty-one percent for McCarthy.

Public reaction to the Kennedy victories was remarkable. The Indiana victory was dismissed by the press as "unimpressive"; the Nebraska victory was termed "inconclusive." Columnists' attacks on Kennedy's character increased in newspapers across the country. Among ordinary citizens, the national hatred of "Bobby" reached such proportions that James Reston in *The New York Times* devoted an entire column to a discussion of it. By comparison, Eugene McCarthy became more and more the shining white knight, clean, pure, and noble. His image remained heroic in defeat as in victory.

This caused the rift between the Kennedy and McCarthy camps to widen at just the moment when unity between them became essential. For during the week between the Indiana and the Nebraska primaries, Hubert Humphrey announced his candidacy, bringing to it the backing of President Johnson and the Democratic Party organization.

In fighting Kennedy, the McCarthy students were in a sense battling their own image in a mirror. In Hubert Humphrey they once again faced the real enemy: the political establishment.

Humphrey, once renowned as a fighter for liberal causes, had now become the administration's chief defender of the Vietnam War. This, coupled with his late entry into the race and the question of whether he was a genuine candidate or a stand-in for a last-minute re-entry of President Johnson, made it almost certain he would lose in "popularity contest" primaries. Humphrey therefore did not enter them. Instead, he sought the support of the political leaders of the regular Democratic Party organizations in nonprimary states. Relying on the "old politics" which enabled a single man—such as Mayor

Daley of Chicago—to deliver the votes of an entire state delegation to the candidate of his choice, Humphrey met with state politicians who controlled all or most of their state's delegates. There were so many of these states, and their combined number of delegates was so huge, that a private poll of convention delegates, taken by *Newsweek* a day after the Nebraska primary, found that Humphrey already had 1279 delegates either pledged to him or "leaning toward" him, while Kennedy had 713, and McCarthy only 280.

Once more McCarthy was asked whether he would withdraw in Kennedy's favor to unite the anti-administration vote. Once more McCarthy said that he would not. The McCarthy movement would continue to fight Kennedy in primaries— while Humphrey went on quietly piling up the delegate votes which would insure his nomination.

Two weeks later, with the Oregon primary, McCarthy's faith in his own candidacy seemed again justified. Oregon, like New Hampshire, had a population literally ninety-nine percent white, and almost entirely middle- and upper-income. As Jack Newfield observed in *Robert F. Kennedy; A Memoir:*

"In beautiful scenic settings, middle-class WASP's just didn't want to hear Robert Kennedy remind them of rat bites in Bedford-Stuyvesant."

The youthful McCarthy crusaders—with signs proclaiming GENE McCARTHY IS A GROOVY TRIP and MAKE THE GENE SCENE—stormed Oregon as they had stormed New Hampshire, and on May 28 Oregon responded by giving McCarthy forty-five percent of their vote to thirty-nine percent for Kennedy. It was McCarthy's first victory over Robert Kennedy; it was to be his last.

On June 4, primaries in South Dakota and New Jersey were to be completely disregarded as the nation concentrated on a third primary to be held in California the same day. The stake for the winner was one hundred and seventy-four delegate votes—the second largest bloc in the country.

California and Tragedy

In no other state are the extremes of American life so glaring or so famous as in California. As the phrase "southern California" connotes swimming pools and canyon homes, plush retirement villages, and the immense wealth and glamor of Hollywood and Beverly Hills, so the word "Watts" symbolizes the desperate frustration of America's black millions. As the San Fernando, San Joaquin, and Sacramento Valleys bring to mind rich farmlands, vast orchards, and wealthy landowners, they also connote the plight of America's exploited migrant farm laborers, who are chiefly Mexican-American. More than any other state, California epitomizes an America in which white affluence and nonwhite desperation became explosively polarized in the Sixties. And it was here that McCarthy and Kennedy arrived for the decisive battle.

In Los Angeles, McCarthy workers opened a discotheque called Eugene's, where Hollywood stars entertained at nightly fund-raising parties. Mr. and Mrs. Paul Newman gave a reception for the candidate and Barbra Streisand was among the guests. In Westwood Village, on the edge of the U.C.L.A. campus, a suburban housewife described her fellow workers at McCarthy headquarters as "college students, educators, and upper-middle-class housewives from Brentwood, Bel Air, and Beverly Hills." And she recorded how delighted she was, as she parked her Buick in front of a department store, to see a McCarthy sticker on a nearby Rolls Royce. California's dissident group, the California Democratic Council, one of the earliest to back McCarthy, gave organization and direction to the campaign and supplied McCarthy with an impressive slate of Congressmen and film stars as delegate-candidates.

Of Kennedy's campaign, Theodore H. White wrote:

"He had seen too many children with bellies bloated by hunger in Appalachia, in Mississippi. He knew of the grape pickers . . . of the unformed yearnings of Mexican-Americans

. . . and when he spoke of the American Indians, of adolescents who hanged themselves . . . he quivered visibly." And White goes on:

"Thus California saw . . . a man whose intensity disturbed their peace. California might . . . see a . . . snatch of a Robert F. Kennedy rally in the deep Negro stretches of Watts, and the emotions he roused threatened peaceful citizens . . . from Beverly Hills to Pasadena. . . . He was the disturber. He meant what he said. . . . If he were elected, he would perform as he promised and the country would change."

Perhaps this is why he had to be killed—as those others who tried to change the country had been killed: John F. Kennedy, Malcolm X, Martin Luther King, Jr. Each had been murdered in the part of the country he had most sought to change: President Kennedy in Dallas, Malcolm X in New York, Dr. King in Memphis. Where should Robert Kennedy so fittingly be killed as in southern California?

He had just time enough to savor a double victory. On June 4, Kennedy defeated both McCarthy and Humphrey in Humphrey's native state of South Dakota. In an Indian district he was charmed to learn that the Indians gave two votes to McCarthy, nine to Humphrey and eight hundred seventy-eight to Kennedy. And he had won the victory that mattered:

By a narrow margin, Kennedy had won California.

At the Ambassador Hotel in Los Angeles, Kennedy supporters gathered for a victory celebration and Robert Kennedy thanked those who had helped him:

"I want to thank all the students who worked across the state. . . ." He still envied McCarthy's loyal army, but he had his own small band of students. "I want to thank Cesar Chavez . . . and all those Mexican-Americans. . . . I want to thank my friends in the black community . . . Rafer Johnson . . . and Rosey Grier, who said that he'd take care of anybody who didn't vote for me."

Then he left the platform and took a shortcut out through

Malcolm X, 1925-1965. *Dan Watts*

John F. Kennedy, 1917-1963. *United Nations*

Robert F. Kennedy, 1925-1968. *United Nations*

Martin Luther King, Jr., 1929-1968. *Dan Watts*

"God, they kill our leaders and they kill our friends."

the kitchen, where an assassin waited for him. Two bullets were fired at Kennedy at close range, one lodging in his brain.

Across the street from the Ambassador Hotel, students ran out of McCarthy headquarters when they heard the news, and their resentment toward a man who had never really been their enemy evaporated in shock. A McCarthy girl, dazed, stood on the sidewalk asking:

"Why? Why another Kennedy?"

Jack Newfield wrote of the college boy with the RFK peace button who was screaming, "Fuck this country! Fuck this country!" Charles Evers, whose brother Medgar had been gunned down a few years earlier, turned to Newfield and said:

"God, they kill our leaders and they kill our friends."

Arthur Schlesinger, Jr. summed up his countrymen more bluntly:

"We are today the most frightening people on this planet."

When the news of Kennedy's death came the next morning, the country was swept by a sense of mass fear and guilt. There was guilt in the realization that the murder of public men had now become commonplace in this once rational country. In the space of five years, two world-famous black leaders and two distinguished Kennedy sons had been cut down by assassins' bullets. And even as Robert Kennedy was being lowered into his grave, Congress was rigidly refusing to outlaw the sale of guns. The mail-order house which had mailed a rifle to John Kennedy's murderer was still free to do a profitable business in murder weapons.

To those close to him, McCarthy seemed to age shockingly in the next few days. He became more withdrawn, more remote, seeming almost apathetic about the campaign as it moved from California to New York.

In the New York primary between Humphrey and McCarthy, which was haunted by the names of Kennedy delegates still on the ballot, apathy was the chief victor: in the most publicized primary in years, a scant twenty-two percent of New York's registered Democrats went to the polls.

Though McCarthy won only fifty-two of New York's one hundred ninety delegates, he won an impressive victory over Humphrey, gaining a majority of the elected delegates. (Nearly a third of New York's delegates are appointed by party leaders.)

With the primaries behind them, the McCarthy crusaders faced the dilemma that had all along been waiting for them. Their candidate had too few delegates committed to him to give him a chance against Humphrey. His only chance lay in winning the support of the delegates who had belonged to Robert Kennedy. And by this time many Kennedy delegates and campaign workers were implacably anti-McCarthy. They bitterly resented the rudeness and contempt with which they had been treated by McCarthy's student campaigners, and the personal attacks McCarthy had made on Kennedy, especially in the last weeks of the campaign. The bitter primary battles had made a real union of Kennedy-McCarthy forces difficult; the assassination made it impossible. If the two forces were to unite against the administration delegates in conventon battles over a Vietnam platform plank, an "open convention," and an end to the old "unit rule," somebody had to be found to represent Kennedy's supporters.

On August 10, less than two weeks before the convention, Senator George McGovern of South Dakota announced that he was a candidate for president. No one took his candidacy seriously; no one was expected to. McGovern had been an ardent Kennedy supporter, but he was also a friend of Eugene McCarthy. His task was to heal the breach between the two camps and unite them, if not behind himself or McCarthy, behind a "dark horse" who might be found at the convention. At the very least, McGovern and McCarthy could unite the "doves" and form a New Politics united front against the administration forces at the convention. Thus, with something like peace between them at last, the two peace camps set out for Chicago and the Democratic Convention, which was to open on Monday, August 25.

The Chicago "Police Riot"

The delegates and alternates were not the only thousands heading for Chicago and the convention. Three other groups, all of them members of youthful movements, were on their way there.

The smallest of the three was the Youth International Party, known as the Yippies. These were the bohemian rebels of the generation, an outgrowth of the "flower people" of the early Sixties, and of the bearded, pot-smoking young of Haight-Ashbury and the East Village, notorious for their "trips" and their love-ins. Lacking the moral purpose of the activists, they specialized in puckish improvised plays and pantomimes, half-solemn political satires accompanied by singing, dancing, and the throwing of flowers. (In Chicago, for instance, they would solemnly dress up a pig as their delegate and propose sending the pig, with flowers to the convention.)

The second group was the Mobilization Committee to End the War in Vietnam. Its leaders included the radicals, but in Chicago, as at the Pentagon, the radicals were a handful; their peaceful antiwar followers, who wanted only to march in an orderly but massive demonstration against the war, were legion.

The third group was, of course, McCarthy's Children's Crusade. McCarthy had urged them not to go to Chicago. He had no real hope of defeating Humphrey and no illusions about Mayor Daley and his police force. (During a ghetto riot following Dr. King's assassination, Daley had ordered his police to "shoot to kill.")

But not even McCarthy could persuade his devoted army to stay home. They had won impressive victories not only for him but for Congressional candidates—such as Allard Lowenstein—running on the McCarthy ticket. Julian Bond, twice denied his seat on the Georgia legislature ostensibly because of his open opposition to the Vietnam War, had been elected a convention delegate on an integrated McCarthy slate. Lowenstein and Bond would be in Chicago to fight for a Vietnam

Yippies protest the "Democratic Circus." *National Guardian*

peace plank. Above all, Senator McCarthy himself would be in Chicago. And who was to say his young crusaders might not somehow pass another miracle for him, and somehow win him the nomination? For eight months, the McCarthy students had worked toward the day of August 25, 1968. Nobody on earth could have kept them from going to Chicago.

So the delegates, alternates, Yippies, antiwar demonstrators, McCarthy students, newsmen, photographers, and magazine writers descended on Chicago.

As the convention opened and the delegates filed in and found the seats allotted to them, one fact became clear. Though he would remain physically absent, President Johnson controlled the convention. His chairman would preside; his hand-picked floor managers controlled the seating of delegates and of visitors in the gallery. As Hubert Humphrey's backer, Johnson did not mean to give the New Politics a forum for their dissent.

California and New York, as the largest delegations, had always been prominently placed near the speakers' platform; this time, the two delegations, with their huge Kennedy-McCarthy majorities, were placed at the very back and at opposite sides of the amphitheatre, as far from the podium and from each other as possible.

Carl Alpert, the chairman, when recognizing delegates who wished to speak, would somehow or other fail to see the McCarthy-McGovern delegates who tried to get the floor. The microphones which connected each state delegation with the podium were controlled by the administration floor managers; and when a McCarthy or McGovern delegate demanded the floor too insistently, his microphone was cut off. One after another, the microphones of dissenting delegations were to be cut off.

Nevertheless, the eight-year moral war being waged by the decade's young activists on three fronts—against the segregationist, military, and political establishments—began to produce results in the workings of the convention's three major committees.

In the Rules Committee, the New Politics delegates demanded an end to the unit rule, by which each delegation cast one vote and the leader of a delegation could bargain away the votes of an entire state. The Humphrey forces, on the defensive against the well-publicized McCarthy prediction of a boss-ruled convention, agreed to replace the unit rule with a one-man-one-vote rule, and the new rule was adopted over the bitter protests of the South.

In the Credentials Committee, another New Politics-Humphrey alignment took place over the angry objections of the South. The committee not only honored the pledge made in 1964 to the Mississippi Freedom Democratic Party, but went further and declared that at future Democratic Conventions no state delegation would be seated whose delegates had been chosen on the basis of racial exclusion or discrimination. The integrated Mississippi Freedom Democratic Party delegation was seated, and the all-white Mississippi delegation turned away. Georgia had also sent rival delegations to the convention: an all-white delegation appointed by party chairmen, and an elected integrated delegation headed by Julian Bond. Each of these delegations was given half of Georgia's seats, but in the future no all-white Georgia delegation would be seated.

In the Platform Committee, the central ideological battle of the convention was being shaped. A Vietnam plank written by the Humphrey majority on the committee was unacceptable to the McCarthy-Kennedy committee members, who wrote their own minority plank. Both majority and minority planks would be presented to the convention for debate.

The majority Humphrey plank stated:

"We reject as unacceptable a unilateral withdrawal of American troops from Vietnam." It proposed an end to the bombing of North Vietnam only when "the action would not endanger the lives of our troops," which presumably left the decision to the generals.

The minority plank called for "an unconditional end to all bombing of North Vietnam" and a "mutual withdrawal of all United States forces and all North Vietnamese troops," to be arranged by negotiations. The two planks were presented to the convention for debate and a vote. The debate, reasoned and instructive on both sides, was broadcast on television and gave the country its first full-scale public symposium on the issue. The vote in the convention resulted in a victory for the Humphrey plank, as predictable as the victory of Humphrey himself, who now had enough delegate votes pledged to him to insure his nomination.

By Wednesday, national attention was focused for other reasons on what was taking place inside the convention. In the convention hall a TV news broadcaster trying to interview a delegate was knocked down and beaten by a Daley security guard; a McCarthy delegate from Connecticut was arrested and hustled off by police on unspecified charges; another McCarthy delegate, a New York housewife, was arrested and held in jail for several hours. When Senator Ribicoff of Connecticut rose to nominate Julian Bond for the vice presidency, Allard Lowenstein attempted to second the nomination, only to find his microphone cut off by the floor manager. As McCarthy and McGovern delegates demanded Lowenstein's right to be heard, the chairman ignored them and plowed on with the roll call as if Bond's name had never been placed in nomination.

But these steamroller tactics were pale reflections of the events taking place in the streets of Chicago, where Mayor Daley's police force was giving the nation a firsthand television glimpse of what an impartial commission later termed "a police riot."

Seven miles from the convention amphitheatre, in and around Grant Park, the anti-Vietnam War Mobilization Committee had assembled its marchers and was waiting for a permit to proceed to the amphitheatre. The permit was denied. Across the street from the park was the Hilton Hotel, where the candidates had their private suites and campaign head-quarters. McCarthy students stood waiting patiently outside the hotel for a glimpse of their hero. (McCarthy, in the traditional manner of candidates, did not attend the convention, but stayed in his hotel room throughout.) Other students came and went, running errands and carrying out assignments from the young workers in charge of McCarthy student headquarters on the fifteenth floor.

The previous night, the leaders of the antiwar Mobilization had been told that Mayor Daley would not give them a permit to march to the amphitheatre. Determined to march anyway, the demonstrators formed ranks in the park. Outside in the streets, the police were also forming ranks.

Suddenly the police charged into the park, clubs swinging, driving the marchers out of the park and into the waiting arms and clubs of larger ranks of policemen in the street.

Wrote John Berendt in *Esquire* magazine:

". . . hordes of policemen charged out of the park into the street, plunging into the crowd and swinging their clubs blindly at people who now had nowhere to go. . . . A boy picked up a handful of stones, threw them, and was fallen upon immediately by seven club-swinging policemen, grunting as they swung with all their might, covering themselves and their nightsticks with blood. A newsman flashed a picture of it and three cops ran at him and pulverized his camera. . . ."

Said a Columbia student:

"I don't see why everybody's so shocked. The cops here don't look any different from the cops at the Pentagon or the cops in Mississippi or the cops at Columbia."

Said French writer Jean Genet:

"The police charged into about 5000 antiwar demonstrators; they did not try to arrest people, but tried to maim people." Genet saw a boy crawling along the gutter, half-conscious and bleeding profusely from head wounds. "A doctor in a white uniform and Red Cross armband began to run toward the kid

Chicago, August 28, 1968: Peace demonstrators battle police and National Guardsmen in Grant Park. *National Guardian*

but two cops caught him from behind and knocked him down. One of them jammed his knee into the doctor's throat and began clubbing his rib cage. . . ."

"You could hear the sodden thuck of club on skull clear up to the fifteenth floor," wrote Jeremy Larner in *Harper's Magazine*. "It was worse than anything I later saw on television. . . . A man tried to carry a bleeding woman into the hotel and they were both clubbed and thrown into the wagon. People ran up to plead with cops beating kids on the ground and the cops turned around and clubbed them. They clubbed men in white who knelt to carry off the fallen and clubbed anyone with a camera."

121

Chicago: The National Guard vs. antiwar demonstrators. *Lee Davidson, LNS*

122

Other writers told of people smashed against buildings, of McCarthy students hurled through plate-glass windows by police and staggering into the fifteenth-floor headquarters with blood streaming from arms, faces, and heads.

In explaining why the Chicago police riot shocked him, Tom Wicker of *The New York Times* explained, by inference, why he and too many of his countrymen had not been shocked or disturbed by police brutality, which by 1968 had become commonplace in most American cities.

"These were not Negroes, rioting and burning in the ghetto," wrote Wicker. These were "the children of affluence." They were white, well-dressed, and well-educated—and because they were, the established order of things "must now justify itself" for attempting to silence their dissent with billy clubs.

Because these demonstrators belonged not to a despised minority but to the affluent white middle class to which *The New York Times* addressed itself, Tom Wicker was shocked. Other newspapers and magazines expressed the same sense of shock. They had hailed McCarthy's student supporters as "the cream of young America," the best the country had to offer. It was not that police brutality could happen here, but that it could happen to *them*. Until Chicago, white, well-to-do citizens (and *Times* reporters) had unconsciously assumed that they were safe, protected by their color, their incomes, and their middle-class status. On the streets of Chicago—and on their home TV sets—they now saw that neither TV commentators nor Red Cross doctors were safe; neither ultrarespectable McCarthy delegates nor young McCarthy students were safe. And if they weren't safe, then nobody was safe.

It was late on Thursday night when the Democratic National Convention ended. On the fifteenth floor of the Hilton, a few students were cleaning up McCarthy student headquarters, rehashing the events of the week and singing a few folk songs to the guitars that had been with them since the

123

New Hampshire primary, staying up through the night before going their separate ways in the morning. Many of them had been together for six months of campaigning.

At four a.m., Chicago police broke into the suite and seized as many students as they could lay hands on, dragging them to the elevator and beating them with clubs on the way down to the lobby. A student who escaped police clutches ran to rouse Richard Goodwin. Goodwin dispatched two students to rouse both Humphrey and McCarthy. Goodwin himself went down to the lobby and casually informed the cops that TV cameramen were on their way, which stopped the police from further beatings until Senator McCarthy arrived. (No one from Humphrey's suite came down to help the students.) McCarthy asked the police to release the students and promised that they would leave Chicago immediately. The cops left, and the McCarthy students packed their bags and left Chicago before another dawn could break on Daley's police state.

So it ended, the high hopeful McCarthy movement and its valiant attempt to recreate the country's corrupt political establishment.

But if McCarthy's candidacy ended in defeat, the achievements of the man and his Children's Crusade remained enormous. A solitary man had challenged the combined might of the political and military establishments; had driven a United States President out of office; and had brought into the political process millions of middle-aged Americans who had until then remained firmly uninvolved, as if "self-government" applied to others but not to themselves. That McCarthy was able to accomplish so much in a little more than a year was due almost entirely to his student army.

If on their first try the student activists failed to destroy the "old politics," it is hardly surprising, nor should it be discouraging. Hopefully, the "crusading children" will return to the political arena for a second try. At the very least, they have demonstrated for future generations the power of the vote, the power of ordinary men and women to change their government and its policies by orderly process at the polls.

Like all the other movements of the Sixties, the impact of the McCarthy movement was greater than the sum of its victories, and will be felt in American political parties long after its defeats have been forgotten.

4

SDS AND THE BLACK YOUNG vs.
THE ACADEMIC ESTABLISHMENT

To the middle-aged American in the Nineteen Sixties, college was what it had been in his youth: an ivory tower in which young people attended classes, joined fraternities, and went to football games, happy to be isolated from the real world in ivy-covered buildings on green campuses; happy to be young (and white), and to submit to the rule of the dean on campus as they submitted to their parents at home. In the Nineteen Sixties, the average middle-aged American knew none of the facts of modern university life.

He did not realize, for example, that many great universities now adjoined vast, poverty-ridden black ghettos and that many students worked in these ghettos. He did not know that many universities were secretly engaged in the development of nerve gases and poison gases for use in Vietnam, and less lethal chemical weapons for use in the very ghettos which were their neighbors.

Nor did the average American have any very clear idea of the power structure of a university. He did not know that presidents of state colleges and universities are appointed and can be removed—by governors and state legislatures, and are therefore under constant political pressure. He did not know that private universities are corporations owned by their trustees, and that these trustees are not educators but successful alumni, many of them executives in the military-industrial complex who naturally use the university to further the ends of that complex.

Nor did middle-aged Americans realize the extent to which many of the younger generation abominated the "double-think" by which their elders lived and by which the universities, owned by their elders, operated. Two examples will describe this "double-think."

In 1962, President Clark Kerr of the University of California at Berkeley welcomed Bishop James Pike to the campus to deliver a speech to the students. On the following day, Kerr cancelled a scheduled speech on campus by Malcolm X—on the grounds that Malcolm X was a religious leader and might proselytize, and that this was forbidden by state law.

To take a more general example, from 1960 onward, black presidents of state-owned Southern Negro colleges were preaching black pride and black equality—while expelling students for sitting in to desegregate all-white restaurants.

Nowhere was "double-think" more evident than in the national attitude toward the young generation of the Sixties. An eighteen-year-old male unable to afford college was an adult, and as such was sent to Vietnam to "fight and die like a man." If his twin brother received a scholarship to college, he was a student, therefore a child, and as such was expected to mind his elders and not trouble himself about the outside world.

Nationally, "double-think" enabled American universities to "have it both ways": to claim tax-exemption as institutions disseminating knowledge for the enlightenment of mankind, while getting lucrative government contracts to develop inhuman war weapons for the destruction of mankind. It enabled universities to invite the CIA and the Dow Chemical Company to recruit students for savagely adult work, and when the students objected, expel them as naughty children.

Another form of "double-think" operated in the university classroom. By the fall of 1967, most American universities had, or were creating, special crash programs to bring more and more black students into college classrooms, where the black students were taught the history, culture, sociology, and psychology of the white race.

These contradictions comprised the root causes of the revolution which in a single year was to bring about a wholesale reformation of the American university structure and university education. The revolution began early in the spring of 1968 and continued through the spring of 1969. Its seeds however, were planted in 1962, with the founding of a national student organization. And a portent of things to come was visible in a single, isolated campus revolt in 1964.

In June of 1962, fifty-nine students from half a dozen colleges met in convention at Port Huron, Michigan, to found a national student organization which they named Students for a Democratic Society (SDS). An offshoot of an old and old-fashioned Socialist organization, the League for Industrial Democracy, from which it immediately broke away, SDS was left-wing in its politics and was to become part of "the New Left." Like all the young movements of the Sixties, SDS was committed at its inception to nonviolence. Its early slogans were "Make love, not war," and "Build, not burn," both indications that SDS would take a leading role in the anti-Vietnam War movement.

With a membership of two hundred students on a few scattered campuses, SDS began by setting up educational centers in big-city ghettos. Its members were to be found on CORE picket lines and at SNCC sit-ins. In 1964, SDS went to Mississippi as volunteers in the COFO Summer Project. By October of 1965, when SDS organized the first large anti-Vietnam War demonstration, its membership had jumped to 6500 students in 150 campus chapters.

The antiwar demonstration led to denunciations of SDS by *Time, Life, Newsweek,* several U.S. Senators, and the Department of Justice. In reply, at a news conference that month, SDS issued a statement of purpose:

"The commitment of SDS and of the whole generation we

represent is clear. We are anxious to build villages; we refuse to burn them. We are anxious to help and change our country; we refuse to destroy someone else's country. . . . We volunteer to go into Watts to work with the people of Watts. . . . We have been risking our lives in Alabama and Mississippi and some of us have died there. But we will not bomb the people, the women and children of another country."

It was in adherence to this credo that SDS became the prime mover in the first half of the student revolution, 1968, and consistently aided the black young who were the prime movers of the second half, 1969. But in 1964, when a "dress rehearsal" student revolt erupted at Berkeley, SDS was still relatively small and unknown.

The Free Speech Movement

Berkeley is one of the campuses of the huge state-owned University of California. It is situated in northern California across the bay from San Francisco, between the two small cities of Berkeley and Oakland. Among the thousands of students returning to the campus in September of 1964 were many who had spent the summer in Alabama and Mississippi with the SNCC-SCLC voter-registration drive. Another group of Berkeley students had spent the summer participating in sit-ins sponsored by the San Francisco CORE chapter to desegregate white businesses and hotels in San Francisco. These students now launched a drive to desegregate public restaurants and businesses in Berkeley and Oakland. One of their targets was the local newspaper, the Oakland *Tribune*.

But since Berkeley is part of a state university, its president is under the control of the governor and the state legislature. And the Oakland *Tribune* was owned by California's most influential elder statesman, former Senator William Knowland. An arch-conservative, Knowland had no intention of altering his hiring policies to please a pack of students.

He was not alone. According to a San Francisco State College professor, the success of CORE student action in desegregating San Francisco's Cadillac outlet and the Sheraton-Hilton Hotel was regarded as "a threat to the white power structure of the entire metropolitan bay area." The white power structure was already fighting back: local ordinances were invoked to make CORE's activities illegal. Sit-ins were "criminal trespass." Picketing was "obstructing traffic" or "obstructing the sidewalk."

Thus matters stood when, in September of 1964, Berkeley students set up SNCC and CORE tables along Sather Way. A mall forming one of the entrances to the campus, Sather Way had been for years the traditional center of student political activity. Since 1964 was a presidential election year, Sather Way was crowded with tables that September. Eighteen organizations had tables there, including Students for Goldwater, Students for Johnson, and Students for Lodge.

But the moment the SNCC and CORE tables appeared, political pressure was brought to bear on Berkeley president Clark Kerr. It was generally assumed to come chiefly from Knowland, but it may have come as well from other white business owners, especially those with political influence. President Kerr suddenly announced that he had just discovered Sather Way was not part of the Berkeley campus, but was on land belonging to the City of Berkeley. Therefore all its tables would have to be removed forthwith.

This caused an uproar on campus. Through the deans who were his spokesmen, Kerr backed down far enough to announce that space would be provided elsewhere on campus for the tables of "qualified" organizations. Questioned about this, the deans defined "qualified" organizations as those which did not collect money for political causes (SNCC was collecting dimes and quarters to send down to dispossessed black families in Mississippi) and those which did not recruit students for off-campus political activity (CORE was recruiting volunteers for sit-ins and picket lines).

But the new rule hampered the presidential campaigners

as much as it hampered SNCC and CORE. Students for Lodge, for instance, were allowed to put up a notice of an off-campus fund-raising rally for Lodge—but were not allowed to mention Lodge's name on the notice, with the result that nobody knew whom or what the rally was for.

By this time all eighteen organizations were up in arms. As one contradictory and confusing rule after another was laid down, revoked, revised, and laid down again by various deans, the eighteen organizations formed themselves into the Free Speech Movement under the leadership of Mario Savio, a philosophy student who had spent the summer in Mississippi. FSM petitions and discussions, and faculty attempts at mediation, all failed to resolve the issue of when and whether Berkeley students were to regain their old freedom of political speech and action.

Meanwhile, SNCC and CORE student volunteers continued to join the picket lines and sit-ins which were attempting to desegregate local businesses, including the Oakland *Tribune*. Students who had withstood the summer-long reign of terror of Southern sheriffs, who had seen their comrades shot and killed and had gone on working in the South, were not likely to be deterred by a city ordinance or a campus ruling. Inevitably, the CORE and SNCC students were arrested by Berkeley and Oakland police for sitting in and picketing. President Kerr thereupon announced that any student arrested by the civil authorities would be additionally punished by the university. This further inflamed the campus and became known as "the double-jeopardy issue."

For three months the dispute dragged on. Early in December, the leaders of the Free Speech Movement staged a sit-in in one of the university buildings and sent a list of demands to the administration, the chief demand being a restoration of the old political freedom. Kerr summoned police to clear the building. In the ensuing "bust," eight hundred students were arrested and an undisclosed number injured. On

Berkeley, California: Mario Savio outside Sproul Hall. *UPI*

the following day, the Berkeley student body went on strike against the university. How little respect existed at Berkeley for the stand the administration had taken may be seen in the fact that the student strike was supported by eighty-six percent of the Berkeley faculty.

The events of the Berkeley revolt and its results formed a pattern which was to be repeated again and again during the nationwide campus revolution in 1968-1969. Unfair as the pattern was, it is hard to see how it could have been avoided. This was the pattern:

(1) Until the sit-in and the police "bust," the day-to-day occurrences at Berkeley had not been news outside the immediate area of Berkeley, Oakland, and San Francisco. (2) Therefore, the newspapers and TV broadcasters reported only that students had taken over a university building and had had to be removed by police. The media accounts condemned the thousands of participating Berkeley students as hippies, narcotics addicts, and Communists, either glossing over the root causes of the revolt or omitting them, possibly from lack of any real knowledge of them. (3) The nation's citizens believed what the news media told them and the general public, too, condemned the student rebels as rioting hippies trying to destroy the university. (4) When the smoke cleared, however, President Kerr and his deans had resigned and the new administration immediately restored to the students the political rights they had demanded in vain during three months of peaceful petition and discussion. (5) Since this news was not headline material, it was buried in the back pages of the press and given just a line on TV news broadcasts, if it was mentioned at all. (6) Thus the nation at large never clearly understood what was at issue, and failed to realize that the students had won a moral victory. The general conviction was that the students were wrong and the establishment right.

It was no accident that the Berkeley revolt had its roots in the Civil Rights struggle. In 1964 that struggle was the overriding national issue. But in the next few years national issues multiplied. In 1965 the national spotlight turned to the war in Vietnam. By 1966 the central issue of the war had widened to include a side issue—the power of the military-industrial complex and its disregard for the international rules of war, which outlaw chemical weapons such as napalm. In 1967 the spotlight switched to the poverty-ridden black ghettos of the North, which that summer were in fierce revolt. By the end of 1967 the Civil Rights struggle, the war, the military-industrial complex, and the plight of the ghettos, were an interwoven tangle of national issues.

The impending student revolution would spring not from one of those issues but from all of them.

Revolt at Columbia *

Columbia University is situated in northern Manhattan in an old rundown residential section called Morningside Heights, and is separated from Harlem by Morningside Park, a city park serving both "the Heights" and Harlem. From ivy-covered dormitory windows above the green campus, Columbia students can look out across the park and see the dark rows of Harlem's tenements. Many students work in Harlem. Many work with the low-income whites, blacks, and Puerto Ricans who live in the old rent-controlled apartment houses and tenements of Morningside Heights. Students at the School of Architecture work on local urban-renewal projects. Students at Columbia Medical School work in the area's clinics and hospitals. Undergraduates in the Collegiate Citizenship Council tutor Harlem schoolchildren. A volunteer teaching corps helps

* The facts used in the present account were taken principally from *Up Against the Ivy Wall,* the remarkable report compiled by Jerry Avorn, Robert Friedman, and their fellow editors of the Columbia *Daily Spectator.* Additional facts were supplied by the personnel of Columbia's radio station WKCR, and by the official report of the Riot Commission appointed to look into the causes of the student revolt.

Harlem High School students, victims of the city's notoriously inferior ghetto schools, to pass college-entrance exams by way of crash courses taught by Columbia students.

To a great many Columbia students, therefore, the residents of Morningside Heights and Harlem were friends, acquaintances, pupils, and neighbors. To the Columbia administration, the people of Morningside Heights and Harlem were roadblocks standing in the way of Columbia's expansion program.

Columbia is a private university, a corporation owned by its twenty-three trustees. In 1968 the average age of these trustees was over sixty; and though they owned a great university, not one of the twenty-three was an educator. They were largely alumni who had become successful corporation executives. They included an investment brokerage head, a CBS executive, the head of a vast real-estate empire, and executives of such formidable members of the military-industrial complex as Con Edison, IBM, Lockheed Aircraft, and Socony-Mobil.

While the composition of its board of trustees was grimly modern, Columbia's method of governing its student body was two hundred years old. In an era when most colleges and universities had long since created faculty-student boards to dispense justice to students accused of misconduct, no such "due process of law" existed at Columbia. Columbia operated on the ancient *in loco parentis* theory, which holds that a university stands "in the place of parents" toward its student children. As the official father, President Grayson Kirk exercised absolute authority; in practice, he delegated this authority to the deans. A student accused of misconduct was summoned to the dean's office; the dean alone heard the student's defense and decided whether to recommend expulsion to Kirk, who alone made the final decision. If the students, being children, were not entitled to "due process" at Columbia, still less were they entitled to inquire into—or judge—the trustees' activities.

By 1967 Columbia's trustees had bought almost all of the land in Morningside Heights. Estimates vary, but a median estimate was that Columbia owned fifty square blocks of apartment houses and tenements, most of which it planned to tear down to make room for new laboratories and dormitories.

This meant that all the apartment-house and tenement families would have to be evicted. But New York City, having a chronic housing shortage, has a law which requires a landlord to find suitable substitute housing for any tenants he wishes to evict. Columbia's trustees consistently broke this law. The university sent illegal, but legal-sounding, letters to tenants ordering them to vacate their homes. Tenants who knew their rights refused to move until substitute housing was found; whereupon Columbia "encouraged" them to move by ripping out heating systems and hot-water systems. In buildings where a few tenants were pressured into moving out and others still refused, rat-attracting refuse was allowed to pile up in empty apartments and superintendent services were reduced or discontinued.

Many Morningside Heights tenants were Puerto Ricans who did not speak English or poor blacks who had no knowledge of their rights. To these, Columbia sent an eviction agent, who threw a hundred-dollar bill at the family, and then pushed the family and its luggage and furniture out onto the sidewalk. If the family had nowhere to go, that was their problem, not Columbia's. If the families turned to Columbia students for help, the administration was not concerned with that either. But it was not the Morningside Heights eviction program which turned Columbia students against the university administration in 1967. It was the plan for a gym in a Harlem park.

Despite the huge amounts of land it owned, early in the Sixties Columbia had decided to build a new university gymnasium—not on its own land but in Morningside Park. Influential trustees had obtained an "enabling act" from the New York State Legislature, giving them the right to lease park land from the city, and had then arranged with the Mayor and the City Council of New York to lease the park land at a low annual rental.

But all that was in the early Sixties. By 1967, when the

architectural plans and financing for the gym were nearly complete, the country had a new awareness of the desperate plight and mood of the ghetto, and New York City had a new mayor. Mayor John V. Lindsay and his parks commissioner, Thomas Hoving, were appalled at Columbia's plan to appropriate public land in one of Harlem's few green parks for a private college gym. Columbia's plan—to use ninety percent of the gym facilities, and leave ten percent for the use of Harlem, the ten percent to be reached by a Harlem back door—was an insult Harlem was not likely to appreciate. Lindsay and Hoving appealed to President Kirk to abandon the gym project. Columbia students also petitioned the administration to build the gym elsewhere. All appeals fell on deaf ears.

That winter Columbia students were exercised about the administration's practice of allowing CIA and Dow Chemical Company recruiters to set up offices on the Columbia campus, where they recruited students on the promise that whose who became couriers for the CIA or helped Dow to invent new napalms would be exempt from the draft. Twice, during November of 1966, SDS led hundreds of students into Low Library, where President Kirk had his offices, to present petitions to Kirk demanding that CIA and Dow be barred from campus offices. Kirk's answer was to ban indoor demonstrations by students.

That was the winter of the phenomenal growth of the antiwar student movement, in which SDS was playing a leading role on every campus. Late that winter SDS uncovered the affiliation of Columbia with the Institute for Defense Analyses and reported this to the Columbia *Daily Spectator*. The *Spectator* checked the story, found it true, and in March of 1967 published the story of IDA.

The Institute for Defense Analyses was a corporation founded in 1956 by five universities, to work on war projects for the Department of Defense, the Department of State, and the CIA. By 1967 IDA had grown to twelve member universities, and its projects included the research and development of new chemical weapons of the napalm-mace variety for use in Vietnam and in "riot control" against American ghettos. Other IDA projects involved atomic bombs and antiballistic missiles. President Grayson Kirk of Columbia was a member of the IDA board; the chairman was William A. Burden, a Columbia trustee.

The multi-million dollar grants from the government enabled member universities to build the new laboratory equipment required for IDA projects, and to pay lucrative side salaries to physics, chemistry, and engineering professors who, as the IDA brochure put it, "work individually at their universities as panel members for the Department of Defense or IDA." (This caused bitter resentment among Columbia's underpaid professors in other departments, since IDA enabled fellow professors to earn double salaries. As a result IDA did much to place many of Columbia's faculty members on the side of the students in the coming crisis.)

To the students of the anti-Vietnam War generation, the news that their university was actively engaged in helping to invent new and deadlier weapons for use in that war was a hair-raising disclosure. More than any other single grievance, it enabled Columbia's SDS chapter to rally and unite large segments of the student community in a war against Columbia.

Under normal conditions, the vast majority of Columbia students disliked SDS. Even those who shared the SDS liberal posture were repelled by the organization's inflammatory style and radical political doctrines. SDS by 1967 had become more and more revolutionary in its politics, and the great majority of Columbia students were political moderates. But the combination of the Morningside Heights evictions, the planned gym in a Harlem park, CIA and Dow recruiting, and now IDA, created conditions which were not normal.

The IDA disclosure came in March of 1967. In April and May student petitions against both IDA and the gym were

139

ignored by the administration. In June the college year ended, and the administration probably assumed the fuss would die down by fall. But the summer of 1967 saw the bloodiest ghetto riots in the country's history. (If they were less severe in New York City than in other American cities it was because Mayor Lindsay had displayed a consistent sympathy and concern for the people of the black community during his first two years in office.)

In the fall of 1967, as Columbia's year of crisis opened, Parks Commissioner Hoving accompanied by such ultrarespectable civic groups as the Friends of Central Park, and by Harlem and Morningside Heights civic leaders, went to Columbia to appeal to President Kirk to abandon the gym project. Politely but firmly, Kirk declined.

On campus the fight against the gym was led by the Student's Afro-American Society (SAS), an organization of black college students founded three years earlier by Columbia student Hilton Clark, son of Negro educator Dr. Kenneth Clark. SAS was joined in its fight against "gym crow" by the Collegiate Citizenship Council and other college organizations, including SDS. Professors and students at the School of Architecture held a "design-in" and submitted blueprints for a new gym to be built on vacant land owned by Columbia. The blueprints, like the petitions and demonstrations, were ignored by the administration.

Then, on February 19, 1968, the Columbia administration lit the first fuse of the explosion to come in April. Construction crews and bulldozers arrived in Morningside Park to clear land for the gym. The next day, Morningside Heights residents and Columbia students turned to one of the standard techniques of nonviolent action: they sat down in front of the bulldozers to prevent construction of the gym from beginning. They were arrested and charged by Columbia with "criminal trespass." A few days later, students and residents joined members of park groups and formed a picket line locking arms and surrounding the gym site. A hundred and fifty people were arrested, more than a third of them students. All were charged by Columbia with criminal trespass.

On campus, the antiwar pressures were increasing. On March 27, in deliberate defiance of the indoor ban on demonstrations, a hundred students marched into Low Library and up to President Kirk's office, demanding an end to Columbia's affiliation with IDA. They were led by the new SDS chapter chairman, Mark Rudd, a junior and a scholarship student at Columbia College. Since the march was a direct defiance of a university rule, all hundred students could now expect to be disciplined by the dean.

A week later, Dr. Martin Luther King, Jr. was assassinated. With the gym construction still going forward, President Kirk and Vice President Truman marched into St. Paul's Chapel to eulogize Dr. King at a memorial service. During the service, Mark Rudd stepped to the microphone and spoke into it to the assembled students.

"Dr. Truman and President Kirk are committing a moral outrage against the memory of Dr. King," Rudd said. He asked how the two men could eulogize Dr. King for nonviolent Civil Rights protest while arresting Columbia students for their nonviolent protest. Branding the service "obscene," Rudd walked out of the chapel, followed by forty other students.

It was at this point that the Columbia dean decided to discipline those students who had defied the ban on indoor demonstrations. But instead of summoning all hundred demonstrators to his office, the dean summoned only six—Mark Rudd, four other SDS officers, and the leader of a campus draft-resisters' organization. All had been in the forefront of the fight against IDA, and they immediately became known on campus as "the IDA six." The second fuse had been lit.

Campus resentment at the university's obvious attempt to silence the six antiwar leaders was widespread. When SDS announced plans for a rally to be held on Tuesday, April 23, more than a thousand students and a sizable number of faculty members turned out for it. As advertised in advance, the rally was to demand justice for the IDA six and an end to both Columbia's IDA affiliation and the gym. Speeches would be heard on all three subjects, after which the rally would become a march to Low Library, where a letter would be presented to President Kirk demanding an open hearing for the six students. These plans were known to everyone, including the administration. When the marchers arrived at Low Library to present their letter they found the library closed and locked.

SDS and SAS leaders now proposed a sit-in in a university building to force the administration to meet student demands for an end to the gym, an end to IDA affiliation, the dropping of criminal charges against the gym demonstrators, and "due process" for the IDA six. Late on Tuesday, April 23, 1968, Mark Rudd of SDS and Bill Sales of SAS led two hundred volunteers into Hamilton Hall. The students locked the dean in his office and "occupied" the building. A committee drew up the list of demands which was sent to the administration. Kirk declined to negotiate with the students, and the sit-ins remained in Hamilton Hall Tuesday night.

On Wednesday SAS sit-ins were visited by Harlem leaders, and when the leaders left the SAS students told the white students they wished to make Hamilton Hall the exclusive symbol of black student protest against the gym. They asked the white students to leave and take over another building. Late on Wednesday night, the white students left Hamilton Hall, broke into Low Library, and occupied the building.

(SDS leaders ransacked Kirk's offices to find proof of Columbia involvement with the Vietnam War. They found documents proving Columbia's ties not only to IDA, but to the CIA and the CIA-affiliated Asia Foundation, including a list of names of possible new presidents of the Asia Foundation submitted to President Kirk by Socony-Mobil. They also uncovered an arrangement made by Kirk with *The New York*

April 23: Mark Rudd speaks at the Sundial rally, flanked by other members of the "IDA six." They are, from left, Ted Gold, Rudd, Nate Bossen, Nick Freudenberg (partially hidden) and Ed Hyman. *David Finck*

April 23: Sitting in at Hamilton Hall. *David Finck*

Times to have the *Times* print an interview with him "putting the gym in a favorable light.")

School of Architecture students working late in Avery Hall that Wednesday night decided to join the sit-in and occupied Avery, claiming it exclusively for architecture students. On Thursday, graduate students occupied Fayerweather Hall. On Thursday night more students took over Mathematics Hall. By Friday morning five Columbia buildings were occupied by sit-ins.

How and why had the administration allowed the "take-over" to spread so far?

A professor who testified later before the Riot Commission pointed out that student sit-ins had occurred earlier at both the University of Chicago and the University of Wisconsin, in which students had occupied a single building and sent a list of demands to the administration. At both universities, the administration had sent negotiators to bargain with the students, a compromise settlement had been reached, the students had left the building, and the incident was over in a few hours. This was one of Kirk's two options. The other was the course taken by Clark Kerr at Berkeley, where a police "bust" had ended the sit-in, also in a matter of hours. However, it had also ended Kerr's career as President of Berkeley.

But to negotiate with Columbia students would have been to treat them as adults. Clinging rigidly to his *in loco parentis* theory, Kirk refused to yield any of his disciplinary authority —even to a faculty committee which attempted to mediate the dispute.

And Kirk had even stronger reasons for not summoning the police. The controversy over the gym and the ghetto riots of the previous summer caused him to fear that a police "bust" involving black students in Hamilton Hall might trigger a race riot in Harlem.

Refusing one option, fearing the other, Kirk delayed and debated in a kind of paralysis—while a full week dragged by.

144

April 28: Passing food into one of the five "liberated areas." *Columbia Daily Spectator*

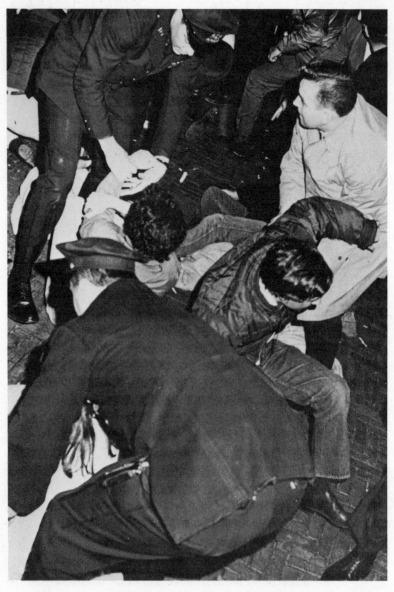

April 30: The bust begins. . . . *Tom Metz*

From April 23 to April 30, five buildings remained occupied, college work came to a standstill, and the faculty committee ran back and forth from the sit-ins to the administration with proposals and counterproposals, all of which failed because Kirk refused to be bound by any agreement reached by faculty and student negotiators. He declined to relinquish his power even to Mayor Lindsay, who offered to mediate the dispute.

On Tuesday night, April 30, just before dawn, the police were summoned. They were ordered not to touch the students at Hamilton Hall, with whom the administration had made a separate agreement. The black students were allowed to leave the building unharmed. Then the "bust" began.

Police broke into the other four buildings in which students had barricaded themselves, and "cleared" them. More than seven hundred students were arrested and a hundred and fifty were injured, in what a *Commonweal* writer and eyewitness called "berserk police savagery." The police smashed young girls against stone walls, clubbed a young rabbi and two professors, injuring them badly enough to send them to a hospital, hurt a *New York Times* reporter, and prevented white-clad internes and nurses from reaching the badly injured who lay bleeding on the campus. One student, his skull split open and his face streaming with blood, was crying in a kind of daze: "Look what the men of this university have done to me!"

(Much was to be made in the press of the damage done to offices and classrooms by the student sit-ins, with particular emphasis on the damage inflicted by SDS on President Kirk's beautiful and expensively furnished office.

(Kirk's office contained priceless oil paintings and nearly priceless carpets, as well as fine mahogany furniture. And the damage caused to it, like the damage caused to other offices and classrooms, resulted from the simple fact that the office had been occupied for a week by a large group of people who had to convert it to living quarters. By the end of the week Kirk's carpets and furniture contained a welter of empty food

147

cartons, milk cartons, coffee containers, beer cans, pop bottles, and emergency medical supplies. The resultant spills, splashes, and spots irreparably damaged the works of art and fine furnishings. But there is little evidence to support the widely publicized suggestion that the damage was wilfully or maliciously inflicted. One professor, angered by press reports, testified that his office was cared for scrupulously by the students and that no damage at all was inflicted until the police moved in and made the office a shambles.)

On the morning of Wednesday, May 1, the mood on the police-occupied campus was grim. Perhaps no date could more effectively have dramatized the difference between college life as middle-aged America remembered it and college life as it was in the Sixties. Thirty years ago, May Day on college campuses was a time of daisy chains and the crowning of May Queens. On May Day of 1968, one Columbia student had had forty-two stitches taken in his scalp where police blackjacks had split it open; five students were hospitalized with injuries; a hundred and fifty bore visible signs of the ferocity of police action in present-day America; eight hundred students were now saddled with criminal police records on complaints filed by the university. Black armbands appeared on campus on May Day morning, worn by students mourning the death of their university.

A strike was called that afternoon. By Friday morning, four thousand students and one hundred and twenty-five professors were boycotting Columbia classrooms, the professors holding classes at their homes or on lawns designated "neutral territory." Many graduate schools continued to function, but the work of undergraduate Columbia College came to a complete halt.

The trustees announced that disciplinary authority was to remain solely in the hands of President Kirk; and that—purely as a courtesy to Mayor Lindsay—gym construction was being "temporarily halted."

The administration point of view was summed up by a trustee later, during the Riot Commission hearings. The trustee was discussing IDA, to which he jovially referred as "Ida." "Ida," he explained, was "a purely corporate function" of the university. It had nothing to do with its academic functions. He repeated the phrase earnestly, over and over, "a purely corporate function!" He was trying to explain that IDA was Columbia's left hand and education was its right hand; he could not understand why on earth the right hand should care what the left hand was doing. To the trustee, this was neither double-think nor hypocrisy; it was the practical principle by which the modern university existed.

This gulf in understanding between administration and student body was highlighted in May when students helped a Morningside Heights Tenants' Action Committee to stage a sit-in in a Columbia-owned building which had had no heat all winter. The tenants still clinging to it lived in a building all but abandoned to falling plaster, uncollected trash, and broken locks. The Columbia administration had all the sit-ins arrested and charged with criminal trespass. Imprisoned in its double-think, the administration could not understand why the students cared about an old Morningside Heights building. It could not understand that to the students a university was a single entity, whose integrity could not be split into moral teaching and immoral "corporate functions."

On May 16, the dean of students announced the expulsion of four of the IDA six. One of the expelled students was Mark Rudd, charged by Columbia with "riot, inciting to riot, and criminal trespass." Ironically, at the very moment of his expulsion Rudd received the official form letter sent to all students who make the Dean's List. The letter began "Dear Mark," congratulated Rudd on his outstanding academic record, and extended the warm wishes of the dean who had just ordered his expulsion. A copy of the letter was being received by Rudd's parents at about the time Columbia was informing his draft board that Rudd was no longer a student and could be immediately drafted for service in Vietnam. (Question: was this an academic or corporate function of the university?)

The news that four students had been singled out for expulsion caused SDS once more to occupy Hamilton Hall to protest reprisals against the four leaders. That night thousands of students gathered on the grounds, waiting for the police "bust." When the police arrived they found not peaceful sit-ins in five buildings as before, but a vengeful mob. Students threw rocks at police cars and set fires in campus buildings. Students and cops together went on a rampage in which sixty-eight more students were injured and one hundred and thirty more arrested. By June, as commencement approached, Columbia had given fifteen percent of its student body criminal police records.

The unsung campus hero during that strange spring term at Columbia was the university's FM radio station, WKCR, operated entirely by students. For two months WKCR's announcers, often on twenty-four-hour duty and going for days without sleep, broadcast continuous bulletins informing students when and where their professors would meet them; broadcast the full hearings of the Riot Commission appointed to investigate the disorders; aired extempore debates between IDA professors and anti-IDA professors, and between SDS/SAS students and a group of conservative right-wing students calling themselves the Majority Coalition. During the explosive one-day sit-in at the end of May, WKCR reporters were stationed at every major spot on campus and broadcast a minute-by-minute account of the second "bust." And in June, WKCR's microphones jumped back and forth to cover the bizarre finale: Columbia's two commencements. Yet never at any time did any WKCR reporter or announcer indicate, by choice of words or voice inflection, whether he had been for or against the sit-ins, for or against SDS or the Majority Coalition. The WKCR staff performed a miracle of unbiased news reportage to make commercial radio and TV stations blush.

Kirk announced that he would not deliver the commencement address as usual; a history professor would deliver it for him. At the same time, three hundred graduating seniors announced that they would not take part in the official exercises but would hold a "countercommencement" on a university lawn. As the regular commencement exercises opened in St. John's Cathedral, the three hundred dissenters rose, filed out of the cathedral by twos, and walked along the campus to their own countercommencement. There in the presence of relatives and friends, they heard addresses delivered by literary critic Dwight MacDonald, philosopher Erich Fromm, and educator Dr. Harold Taylor, former President of Sarah Lawrence College. All three were middle-aged. All were distinguished members of that unpublicized alliance between the student activists and their over-forty admirers.

The events at Columbia repeated the Berkeley pattern. The student takeover of five buildings and the police "bust" had made front-page headlines across the country, but had also been the first news the country had of any trouble at Columbia. Newspapers and TV broadcasts condemned the Columbia "riots" as a massive uprising of unruly, irresponsible children led astray by the radicals of SDS. Press and public united to condemn the rebels.

The rest of the story did not make headlines.

In June of 1968, Columbia announced that it had severed its affiliation with IDA. In July President Kirk and Vice President Truman resigned. In July and August a student-faculty committee worked out a "restructuring" of the university, to provide "due process" for all students accused of misconduct and a student voice in the governing of the university. In February, 1969, Columbia's new administration announced the permanent abandonment of the plans for a gym in Morningside Park. During the fall months, criminal charges against eight hundred Columbia students were quietly dropped. Only in the expulsion of the four students did the university refuse to yield. Every other student demand had been fully met.

The size and scope of the Columbia revolution made the very word "Columbia" a synonym for campus rebellion. SDS at other colleges began to call for "more Columbias." The news media accused students of other campuses of "trying to bring about another Columbia." (This might have given Americans pause, had they ever been taught in school that during the American Revolution, the not-yet-named United States was called "Columbia" by its rebelling patriots.) But if Columbia triggered the wave of student revolts which swept the campuses in the following college year it was by no means the cause of them.

The Revolution Spreads

The Columbia revolt ended in June of 1968, a month when thousands of students across the country were working in Eugene McCarthy's primary campaign. For these students the summer of 1968 began with the assassination of Robert Kennedy and ended with the police bloodbath at the Democratic Convention in Chicago. In September, battle-scarred and disillusioned, having lost their long fight to elect a "dove" presidential candidate, they returned to college to find their college administrations helping the military-industrial complex to recruit students for the Vietnam War. The revolt which followed was inevitable.

It began with widespread campus revolts against ROTC, the Reserve Officers' Training Corps. Students who passed campus ROTC courses became reserve officers in the army or navy and were exempt from the draft, subject to only a few weeks' military service each year on this side of the water. As an added inducement, they received academic credit for their ROTC training. Officers in charge of ROTC were given faculty status for their work. This meant that the higher a university's academic standards, the more bitterly did students and faculty alike resent the granting of academic credit and faculty status to the ROTC.

In the winter and spring of 1968-1969, student petitions and demonstrations calling for an end to ROTC took place at Dartmouth, Harvard, Michigan, Princeton, Purdue, Stanford, Wisconsin, and uncounted lesser-known colleges where academic standards were high. By the end of the year three of the Ivy League colleges—Columbia, Harvard, and Princeton—had responded by abolishing ROTC on their campuses. Many of the other colleges put an end to academic credit for ROTC trainees and academic status for instructors, and ROTC became just one more extra-curricular activity, diminished in both size and importance.

At the same time, SDS chapters were leading the anti-IDA fight at affiliated universities. At Stanford, the university finally bowed to campus protest and severed connections with IDA. At the Massachusetts Institute of Technology, which, largely through IDA, received more government war-related contracts than any other university in the country, student action resulted in an announcement at the end of the year by the M.I.T. administration that the university was discontinuing seventy-five percent of its government contracts, including its affiliation with IDA. According to one report, by June of 1969 the drive against IDA had reduced the number of its member universities from twelve to five.

At the same time, campus revolts against the CIA and Dow Chemical Company recruiters spread with renewed force. In April of 1969, demonstrations against the CIA and Dow Chemical reached even the staid campus of Notre Dame, the country's most famous Roman Catholic university and a traditionally conservative stronghold. That April, students of Notre Dame lay down in the lobby of a building to block the entrance to CIA offices set up in it. Father Hesburgh, the priest who was president of Nôtre Dame, thereupon issued an edict:

"Anyone or any group that substitutes force for rational persuasion, be it violent or nonviolent, will be given fifteen minutes of meditation to cease and desist" or face expulsion.

President Nixon sent Father Hesburgh a letter congratulating him on his edict. And two hundred American newspapers printed editorials praising Father Hesburgh for his stand. The *Manchester Guardian,* official organ of Great Britain's Liberal Party, took a different view.

Reminding readers that "all that the revolutionaries had done was to lie down in the lobby of a building in which a CIA talent scout was conducting interviews, and invite students who wanted a job to trample on them the way the CIA trampled on the rights of small countries," the *Guardian* asked:

"Instead of telling the national press how such mild-mannered would-be martyrs would be punished, should not a Christian university ask whether it really wanted to smooth the path of intelligence agents and napalm manufacturers by allowing them to recruit on its premises?"

The clergymen who ran Notre Dame did not ask this question. Fortunately for the future of Christianity, their students did.

A revolt, however mild, at conservative Notre Dame might have startled the press and public into taking a sober look at the causes behind the student movement, but it did not. It remained for another college to jolt a small segment of the press and public into a grudging reappraisal of student unrest. That college was Harvard.

Harvard is unique among American educational institutions. For more than two centuries it has been the country's undisputed symbol of intellectual supremacy. Only the best young minds of each generation are accepted there; only the most distinguished names in the arts, sciences, and professions join its faculty. When the news broke of a student sit-in, a police "bust," and a strike of seventy-five percent of the students supported by many members of the faculty—at *Harvard*—even the most respectable and conservative of the nation's magazines were distinctly jolted.

The week following the trouble at Harvard, *Time* magazine devoted its cover and several closely packed pages to the causes, as well as the actions, of the Harvard revolt. The account revealed close similarities between the events at Harvard and at Columbia. Student resentment had been aroused at Harvard by administration plans to expand its Medical School by tearing down housing in the nearby black ghetto of Roxbury, and by Harvard Corporation involvement with the Vietnam War. There was in addition a special resentment of ROTC at Harvard, where academic standards were higher than anywhere else in the country.

When petitions and demonstrations failed to get any action, SDS led two hundred and fifty Harvard and Radcliffe students into an administration building, took over the administration offices, and evicted the deans. A list of demands was sent to President Pusey, after which SDS leaders ransacked university offices for proof of Vietnam War contracts. According to *Time*, they uncovered letters which revealed "close ties between Harvard facultymen and the CIA, the Defense Department, and the State Department," which suggests IDA. The administration responded to the students' demands by summoning police. Four hundred state troopers and police arrived on campus and attacked both the crowds of students outside the building and the sit-ins. Fifty people were injured, one woman suffering a broken back. At Harvard, as at Columbia, the student body at large was stunned by the "bust" and called a three-day strike against the university.

A few weeks later, in a rare example of academic common sense, President Calvin Plimpton of Amherst College joined with his faculty and student body in convening a two-day "teach-in" to debate, discuss, and explore the causes of the current student revolution. The result was a letter sent to President Nixon and released to the press, signed by Plimpton, faculty, and students, and referred to in the press as "the Amherst Declaration." The letter asked President Nixon to realize that student unrest had its roots in moral outrage and moral frustration, and would continue until "political leadership addresses itself to the major problems of our society—the huge expenditures of our natural resources for military purposes, the inequities practiced by the present draft system, the critical needs of America's twenty-three million poor, the unequal division of our life on racial issues."

This time even *The New York Times*, in praising the Amherst Declaration in an editorial, gave recognition to the fact that the college generation was trying not to destroy American universities but to reform them.

But the real reformation was yet to come. The student revolts so far had all been directed at university involvement with the Vietnam War and its mistreatment of nearby ghettos —at the nonacademic, "purely corporate" functions of the university. They were to form only the first and less important phase of the student revolution, since they dealt with current, temporary situations and crises.

The second, and most important phase of the student revolt, which reached its height in the spring of 1969, was aimed at the university classroom itself—the curriculum, teaching methods, and admissions criteria of American universities. This movement was the work of the black young, who were to move and shake the American educational system to its foundations.

The Black Studies Movement

"The universities," remarked Negro psychiatrist Dr. Price M. Cobbs in February of 1969, "have become the dusty

Southern towns of today." He might have been speaking about the entire American educational system, from kindergarten through college.

The American educational process begins with standard IQ tests given to five-year-old kindergarten children to gauge their general intelligence. In one of these tests, a child is shown photographs of two faces and asked to say which is prettier. Both faces are white, but one face has white characteristics— straight nose, thin lips, a frame of soft hair; the other has Negroid features—broad flat nose, full lips, and African hair. If the child chooses the white-featured face as prettier, he has answered the question correctly.

"This shows," commented Dr. Gloria Joseph, Cornell psychiatrist, "that our society feels that by the age of five a child should have internalized the white concept of what is prettier."

The education of a black American child thus begins with a brutal white test designed to teach the child that he or she can never hope to be handsome. Through grade school and high school, the black child is taught from textbooks written by and for whites, in which the black race is either never mentioned or mentioned briefly with contempt. A black college student testified that in the midwestern high school from which she graduated in 1966, her race was referred to only in photographs of slaves "which showed us all picking cotton and shuffling our feet." A white teacher in a Harlem high school put it more succinctly. Speaking of the history and social studies books used in her school, she said:

"These textbooks say to the children in my classroom: 'You don't exist.'"

Today, as in Malcolm X's school days, when black students reach their junior year in high school many white teachers try to discourage them from taking college-preparatory courses, on the theory that for blacks the only "realistic" goal is a trade. A student at the University of the City of New York who had graduated from a ghetto high school in 1968 testified that

157

throughout his school career, white vocational counsellors consistently tried to talk him out of going on to college.

For those black students who, despite such indoctrination and discouragement, went on to college, the end of the educational process proved to be no different from its beginning. In college, as in grade school and high school, they were taught by white professors using textbooks written by and for whites and presenting the white man's view of sociology and psychology, the white man's economic structures, and the history of the white man's culture and civilization.

It was this consistently racist educational system which became the target of the black college generation in 1968 and 1969. Professor Charles Hamilton, Chairman of the Political Science Department of Roosevelt University in Chicago, asserted that the black student revolt had its roots in the disillusionment which followed the Mississippi Summer Project. That project had been an effort on the part of young black Americans to gain the simplest rights of white society, and so join it. When the effort was met with murder and violence at the hands of white sheriffs and police chiefs, and their actions were sanctioned by white state governments and allowed to go unpunished by the federal government, the black young lost all desire to become a part of such a society. They determined instead to build their own black society.

But other forces were also at work during the Sixties to shape the black young. Malcolm X had come and gone, bequeathing to the teen-agers of the Sixties a legacy of black pride and black self-esteem. He had proclaimed to these young Americans that black was beautiful; he had told them of great nonwhite civilizations deleted from white textbooks; he had given America's black young a sense of identity with the countries of "the Third World."

To Malcolm's influence was added the equally profound influence of Dr. King. As small children, the black college generation of 1969 had seen King's nonviolent techniques win for black Americans equal rights on public buses and in public restaurants, in public parks and libraries. It was natural that they should grow up to demand equal rights in their own world of the classroom.

The event that triggered the Black Studies movement was the assassination of Dr. King in April of 1968. However, the movement would have been impossible even three years earlier. A movement, after all, requires numbers, and until 1968 there were not enough black students on major American campuses to make an educational revolution possible.

During President Johnson's administration the government had instituted the Equal Opportunities Program, designed to give more black high-school graduates a chance at a college education by providing federal funds for the setting up of special crash programs for incoming black freshmen, whose inferior ghetto schooling had not prepared them for college. The crash programs were financed by federal grants to state- and city-owned colleges; many private colleges received foundation grants for the same purpose. Such programs were set up at colleges all across the country, under a variety of titles. At Cornell, it was COSEP—Committee on Special Educational Projects—financed by the Ford Foundation. At New York's City University, it was SEEK—Search for Education, Evaluation, and Knowledge—financed by government funds.

As a result, black students were arriving at American colleges in greater numbers than ever before. Once there, they began to ask embarrassing questions. Why did their college courses include no history of their own race and culture? Why were there no psychology or sociology courses dealing with the causes and effects of white racism? Why were there no economics courses relating to modern urban problems and the economic dilemma of the ghetto? The embarrassing questions were met with silence or evasion from college administrations. The black students' questions became petitions for Black Studies courses. The petitions went unanswered, and gave rise to a new movement.

To launch their Black Studies movement, the students

159

formed their own college organizations. At Berkeley it was the Black Students' Union. At Wisconsin it was the Association of Black Students. At Notre Dame and several Eastern Ivy League colleges it was the Students' Afro-American Society, founded at Columbia in 1964—though each SAS operated independently of the others and of the original SAS. In April of 1968, these and similar black student groups began petitioning their college administrations for courses in Black Studies.

Berkeley led the way. With SDS backing, two black student groups demanded and got five Black Studies courses added to the Berkeley curriculum by the fall of 1968. Most universities, however, dragged their heels, ignoring or evading student petitions through the winter of 1969. It was only after months of fruitless petitioning that the black students in the spring of 1969 turned to nonviolent action, and a wave of demonstrations, sit-ins, and classroom boycotts swept the country, beginning in February and continuing through June. Said a New York City College student after a black students' strike there brought classes to a halt:

"The major political lesson I have learned from this strike is that to get any attention from a bureaucratic structure you have to hit that structure over the head. We petitioned for months and nothing happened. It was only when we locked up the campus that things happened."

At Notre Dame, where the athlete is king and black athletes are often campus idols, SAS staged demonstrations at football games. When plans were announced to continue the demonstrations at a coming basketball game, the administration appointed a student-faculty committee to set up a Black Studies program at Notre Dame by 1970.

At San Francisco State College, months of fruitless petitioning for a Black Studies Department led, in November of 1968, to a student strike. The strike dragged on for months, and was met by constant police action. After one police "bust," a reporter for the *Daily Californian* found on the campus lawn

San Francisco State: One student down . . . *LNS*

161

San Francisco State: . . . and more to go. *LNS*

"tiny homemade crosses marking the dried pools of blood" shed by students at police hands.

At Wisconsin State University at Oshkosh, and at San Fernando Valley State College in California, the depth of white racism proved ugly indeed. Both colleges were state-owned, supported by black as well as white taxpayers; but both for years had been almost exclusively white. Under the Equal Opportunities Program, both were now forced to admit black students.

At Wisconsin State, one hundred and three black students were admitted, and petitioned the university for Black Studies courses without success. Ninety of the black students finally staged a one-day sit-in in an administration building. The Wisconsin State Board of Regents promptly expelled all ninety students; and the thirteen uninvolved black students seemed unlikely to remain, so violent was white campus reaction against them.

At San Fernando Valley, after black students unsuccessfully petitioned for a Black Studies program, twenty-seven of them attempted to dramatize their demands by holding a four-hour sit-in in an administration building. According to the Catholic weekly *Commonweal*, President Blomgren called in the police, who took over the campus and "established a virtual reign of terror . . . upon every black student on campus." The black sit-ins were arrested, and their bail set so high that they were forced to stay in jail. San Fernando's all-white faculty demanded the expulsion of the black students and booed the few white professors who pleaded for fairness. Governor Reagan appointed a grand jury to inquire into the four-hour sit-in, and the grand jury returned an indictment charging the twenty-seven sit-ins with "kidnapping, burglary, and robbery." California newspapers hailed Reagan and the grand jury. At present writing, the fate of the twenty-seven could not be learned.

At Southern University in Baton Rouge, Louisiana, the country's largest Negro university, student petitions for Black Studies failed to get action, and the students called a twelve-day boycott against the university. When this, too, failed, students held a symbolic forty-five minute sit-in in administration offices and then adjourned to the auditorium for a rally. To "quell" this "disturbance," Louisiana Governor McKeithen ordered five hundred state troopers to the campus and expressed the hope that the president would "expel those students . . . and any faculty members who aided . . . this what you might call insurrection."

But if racism triumphed in small state colleges in bigoted Wisconsin and California towns as well as in a large university in the Deep South, the Black Studies movement was winning major victories in almost all of the country's leading universities. By the end of the college year, Black Studies Institutes or Departments were scheduled to open in 1970 at Ivy League Columbia, Cornell, Harvard, Penn, Princeton, and Yale, and at major state colleges and universities from Berkeley and San Francisco to the University of Minnesota and New York University. Many of the best small private colleges followed suit, including predominantly Quaker Swarthmore, predominantly Jewish Brandeis, and predominantly Catholic Notre Dame and Fordham. This is merely a partial list, to which more colleges and universities are being daily added at present writing.

Inevitably, the Black Studies movement exposed the depth of the nation's white racist educational system and its effect on the students and professors who were products of it. At Harvard, the first Black Studies courses begun in the spring of 1969 were taught by white professors who, as a black senior put it wearily, were "blissfully unaware that their bigoted and paranoid outlook makes a shambles of scholarship." The demand arose for black professors to staff the new Black Studies school.

At Cornell, students demanded a voice in the selection of the man to head the new Black Studies school and the men to staff it. The Cornell story deserves special notice. It contains within itself the history of the Civil Rights movement, the depth of American white racism, and the clash when the two meet head-on.

The current Civil Rights movement began after the 1954 Supreme Court decision, with the enforced integration of Central High School in Little Rock, Arkansas. One of the leaders of the Black Studies movement at Cornell was Ed Whitfield, Cornell class of 1970, a black alumnus of Little Rock Central High School, where he graduated fifth in a class of six hundred. Leading the SAS revolt against Cornell's white-oriented curriculum and the racial bias of its white textbooks and professors, Whitfield pointed out that such bias distorted the teaching of sociology, psychology, political science, and economics. It was for this reason that SAS students at Cornell demanded a voice in the selection of the Black Studies staff.

Traditionally an exclusive white college, Cornell was bound to have not only the radical liberals of SDS and SAS but conservative fraternities, some of them bitterly antiblack. Late in April, 1969, trouble erupted. White fraternity students burned a cross on the lawn of Wari, the residence of thirteen black Cornell girls. The cross-burning, with its nightmarish connotations of the Ku Klux Klan, was accompanied by anonymous obscene phone calls to the girls. At the same time, anonymous calls were threatening the SAS leaders with death.

A week later, during Cornell's Parents' Week, a group of SAS students walked into an administration building, evicted visiting parents and college officials, and occupied the building, to press their demands for black representation on the student-faculty disciplinary board. That evening the girls at Wari received anonymous phone calls informing them that carloads of fraternity boys were on their way to Wari to "take care of" the girls. Similar phone calls to the administration building told the SAS sit-ins that carloads of fraternity boys were coming to "free" the building, and that the fraternity boys were armed. The black students phoned friends outside who brought them guns and rifles with which to defend themselves. When the administration learned of a potential armed confrontation between black and white students, negotiators were sent to the administration building, an agreement was quickly reached, and the sit-in ended.

The nation's press shouted the headlines that the Cornell administration had "capitulated" to black students "at gunpoint." In a country where the possibility of black men arming themselves had been a paranoid white fear for three centuries, the incident brought the nation's deepest fears and bitterest prejudices to the surface. The reaction was intensified when in New York City, racial clashes broke out at the Queens, Brooklyn, and City College campuses of the City University.

Cornell: Black students on guard at 320 Wait Hall, the Afro-American
Society center. *Cornell Daily Sun/LNS*

166

New York's City University is a vast complex of four-year academic and two-year community colleges supported by state and city taxpayers. But the daytime enrollment of its leading four-year academic colleges—the three aforementioned—has for years been almost entirely white. New York's black and Puerto Rican children were products of the city's ghetto schools, which scarcely fitted them for college. But the SEEK program brought large numbers of both groups to the three campuses, and in the spring of 1968 black and Puerto Rican students began to petition the university for Black Studies programs. As the City College student quoted earlier said, they "petitioned for months and nothing happened."

In January, the SEEK students at Queens took over the faculty dining hall and library and reportedly smashed the contents of both in a destructive rampage. Not until then did the white majority at Queens College even know that the black students had been petitioning for anything. The white students had pretended that the black students didn't exist.

"I come here every day," said one black Queens student, "and it's as if they look right through me. No one knows me or talks to me." He was one of a thousand black students on a campus of 26,000.

At City College, black students who had petitioned the administration for nine months without results were making demands which were both radical and farsighted: (1) a required course in Black History and in the Spanish language for all students majoring in Education—since those students were the ghetto schoolteachers of the 1970's; (2) the admission of black and Puerto Rican high-school graduates to City College in proportion to their numbers in the city's high schools. When petitioning failed, the SEEK students, with the help of SDS, called a strike, and forced its effectiveness by blockading the college's South Campus. The strike and blockade brought the work of the college to a halt.

It was only then that the white majority was forced to face

Queens College: A rally in support of the SEEK students. *Howie Epstein, LNS*

the fact of black students' existence, since the black and Puerto Rican minority was now preventing the white majority from attending classes. The white students reacted violently.

On the predominantly Jewish campus, racial bias between Negroes and Jews was particularly bitter. There were open clashes between SDS and SEEK students on one side, and student members of the Jewish Defense League on the other. Police summoned to prevent further violence added to it; the college closed down in a blare of headlines and violent anti-black public reaction.

But when a new president took over at the college and it reopened, there was a hopeful aftermath, reported fully in the New York *Post*. Student leaders, with the approval of the new president, organized a two-day "teach-in" in which black and white students finally talked about the problem face to face. One exchange between a black and a white student, as reported by the *Post*, exposed the root of the problem.

Said the white student, discussing the demand that black and Puerto Ricans be admitted in proportion to their high-school numbers:

"I am white and if that means that white students are going to be taken out of City (College) or not admitted . . . to make way for black students, then I will fight it."

To which the black student replied:

"We have been discriminated against for two hundred years, and now maybe you will have to be discriminated against to give us a chance to make up for all we never had. Many of you whites can afford to go to other universities, but we can't afford to, we have to go here, and we want a quota system to insure that we do."

In the virulent antiblack sentiment which swept the city as a result of the university disorders, few people noticed that the Black Studies movement had chalked up another victory. Black History and Spanish language courses will henceforth be required subjects for all education majors at City College;

and a quota of black and Puerto Rican students equal to their numbers is being established through an Open Enrollment Plan to go into effect in 1970.

With the number of new Black Studies Schools multiplying at universities across the country, a hunt was now on for qualified black professors to staff them. This led to a "brain drain" on the state-owned Negro colleges of the South. Those colleges were staffed by professors who had been traditionally excluded from the faculties of both private and state-owned universities because of their color. Now, suddenly, they were in demand at the country's finest universities. They began to leave their poorly paid, rigidly censored and controlled teaching posts in the South to go north and west to the new Black Studies Schools.

But the brain drain must be temporary. The new Black Studies Institutes will in a few years graduate a generation of young black professors whose numbers should increase dramatically in the next decade. Given the deep commitment to their people of today's black young, it is probable that many of the new professors will go south to teach in the Negro colleges where they will be needed.

A Decade Ends

The last year of the Sixties was the most revolutionary year of the decade; and revolutions are hard on those who live through them. At the end of a year of unremitting and unprecedented campus revolts, the country not surprisingly "overreacted."

In the California State Legislature, more than a hundred separate bills were introduced designed to stifle student dissent by such devices as cutting off state aid and state scholarships to all students who participated in campus protest. In New York, one state legislator declined to guess the number of laws already passed to the same end, or the number of bills still pending. He explained that each fresh student demonstration or sit-in anywhere in the state had brought a new flood of bills, each with a new definition of what constituted student "crime." New laws declare that students engaging in protests in any college or university in the state of New York will lose their regents' scholarships, their government grants or loans, their SEEK or other Equal Opportunities Program benefits, and their draft deferments. A Civil Liberties Union lawyer privately expressed the belief that most of these hastily drafted anti-student laws would prove unconstitutional if tested in the courts, but it is to be hoped that such tests will not be necessary. It is not an unrealistic hope.

The student rebels of the Sixties were neither irresponsible nor unreasoning. Their grievances were real and profound; and they turned to building takeovers and student strikes only when every other more peaceful means had failed to move intransigent administrations. In winning the major reforms they demanded, the students of the Sixties may have paved the way for more flexible college administrations who will be responsive to peaceful petitions in the future. They may even have made such petitions unnecessary—except in those colleges where all student appeals for reform fell on deaf ears, as at Wisconsin State and San Fernando Valley. Where there are no real grievances, there is no student revolt. Proof of this was demonstrated at Columbia where, in the spring of 1969, new and irresponsible SDS leadership attempted to manufacture a second revolution on flimsy grievances. The attempt fizzled out overnight for lack of student support.

Meanwhile, the positive results of the student revolution are impossible to overestimate, particularly with regard to the Black Studies revolution. Within a few years, universities will be graduating young teachers who will be the first to enter American grade-school and high-school classrooms with a knowledge of, and respect for, the history and culture of their black students as well as white. Black Studies Institutes will graduate a new breed of American psychologist who will outlaw IQ tests imposing white standards of beauty on black children, and a new breed of sociologist equipped to teach the cause and effect of racism. There will be a new breed of historian whose textbooks will tell the truth about the slave trade, about the deliberate white extermination of America's native Indian population, and about American treatment of its Chinese and Japanese minorities—thus putting America's racism in perspective and relegating racist educational doctrines to the past. For the first time it is possible to believe that American children will, in the foreseeable future, receive an education through which children of all races will learn to respect each other. In this projected reformation of its educational system, begun by the black young of the Sixties, lies the country's only hope of racial peace and justice.

It is fitting that the stormy decade, which opened with the polite request of four black college students for a cup of coffee at Woolworth's, should end with the prospect of an American educational system in which children will one day read in American history books the story of those four students.

EPILOGUE

December, 1969

Six days before the end of the decade, the book is finally finished.

On the author's desk is a clutter of newspaper clippings collected at random during the past few weeks. Few of the news items made the front page. Most of them might easily escape notice—especially the notice of millions of newspaper readers who have roundly condemned the student activists of the Sixties.

One item, for example, concerns a speech delivered at a political dinner in New York by Charles Evers, brother of the murdered Medgar Evers. The item states that Charles Evers, who is black, was recently elected Mayor of Fayette, Mississippi. Another clipping gives small, neat headlines to the fact that the voters of Atlanta, Georgia, have just elected a black Vice-Mayor. Alongside these two clippings is a letter from SCLC announcing that black candidates have been elected to a majority of local offices in Greene County, Alabama, on the Mississippi border.

The few front-page news stories concern the October 15 Vietnam War Moratorium Day. According to the newspaper accounts, the Moratorium Day was originally planned by the nation's college students as an observance to take place on campuses across the country. But so many middle-aged citizens clamored to take part that the ceremonies had to be transferred from college campuses to the main streets, parks, and cathe-

Moratorium Day (October 15, 1969) in New York City. *Dan Watts*

174

Moratorium Day: At San Francisco State, caskets draped with NFL and American flags and thousands of crosses were placed on the campus lawn. *LNS*

drals of major American cities. In New York City, the Moratorium Day observances had the full support of Mayor John V. Lindsay—himself the subject of another set of clippings.

The Lindsay story made front-page headlines in New York and was an important news story in most of the country's major cities. The news was that Mayor Lindsay had been reelected despite the fact that he was not the candidate of either the Republican or the Democratic Party. Newspaper editorials and television news commentary stressed the fact that the two major parties seemed to have lost their traditional hold on the voter.

175

A final handful of clippings contains small, random news items from the campus:

Columbia University has just announced an end to life terms for its trustees. Henceforward, Columbia trustees will be elected to limited terms in order "to infuse new blood and new ideas" into the university administration.

Cornell has appointed an ombudsman to relay student grievances to the faculty and administration. Through regular meetings, the ombudsman will keep each of the three groups in close contact with the other two.

Tufts College in Massachusetts was given modest headlines for its action in filing suit against the local building-construction unions. Tufts wants the court to force the unions to admit black construction workers before beginning work on a federally financed Tufts dormitory. The court case is expected to have wide repercussions, since a favorable decision for Tufts could force construction unions throughout the country to open their doors to black members.

None of these items is of major importance except, perhaps, to the young activists who suffered so much—and have been so much maligned—in their efforts to bring about such small, historic changes. Perhaps it is wishful thinking, but to one citizen it seems that as 1969 closes the moral revolution undertaken by the young reformers of the Sixties has clearly borne fruit.

It has borne fruit in the South in new voting patterns and in the continued desegregation of public facilities. It has borne fruit in the growing ranks—and the growing respectability— of the anti-Vietnam War movement, which is no longer confined to the younger generation. It has borne fruit in a growing refusal of the average voter to accept the anachronistic organization and thinking of the two major political parties. Above all, it has borne fruit in the wholesale reformation of American university life.

If the American establishments—political, military, and

176

white racial—remain corrupt, violent, and intransigent in too many areas, their complacent belief in their own impregnable power is gone. From the White House to the Pentagon, from the local polling booth and lunch counter to the local college boardroom and classroom, the power of the establishment has been challenged successfully, and it has proved vulnerable indeed to genuine and sustained demands for reform. But the demands must be sustained in the decade to come if they are to be permanent. Establishments, like the men who form them, do not stand still: if they are not pushed forward they will slide back.

It is no secret that university administrations, which gave in to demands for reform only under intense student pressure, secretly hope to reverse themselves as soon as the pressure relaxes. Nor will the major political parties allow another McCarthy to rise if they can stop him.

"Eternal vigilance" is still the price of liberty for black America, and of freedom of thought and action for those who challenge the status quo in a university or at a political convention.

And the task of being eternally vigilant in the cause of moral reform must be borne chiefly by the young; for only youth has no one but itself to consider. A man who depends upon the military-industrial complex for the salary that feeds his wife and children cannot afford to become a crusader. If he loses his job, his wife and children may starve. A professor who crusades for university reform may lose the promotion and pay rise he counted on to pay his children's doctor bills. A few gallant and self-sacrificing men and women in the older generation can always be found to risk and lose everything for a moral cause; but they are few. The real burden of reform, of righting the wrongs of their society, must fall upon the young.

This obligation, discharged with so much valor and honor

by the young activists of the Sixties, now devolves upon the young of the Seventies. Nor is the task of reforming American society less urgent today than it was ten years ago.

Black America is still not free to live where it pleases, work where it pleases, vote in Southern elections, or obtain an unbiased and adequate education for its children anywhere in the country. The war in Vietnam is not over. The major political parties still do not mean to obey the will of the people if, by fair means or foul, they can thwart that will at national conventions. And the reformed university corporation, like the new Black Studies Institutes, will last just so long as students demand them and no longer.

This is the many-sided challenge which now confronts the young activists of the Seventies. To them, the movers and shakers of the Sixties have bequeathed high moral goals to shoot at and a shining example of selflessness and courage to follow.

But whether there will, indeed, be young activists in the Seventies, and whether they will pursue the same goals as their predecessors, no one can say. In the history of American decades no two have borne any similarity to each other. What the Seventies will be like is a question only the Seventies can answer.

A SELECTED
BIBLIOGRAPHY

BOOKS
ON THE BLACK REVOLUTION (SNCC)

Chambers, Bradford (editor), *Chronicles of Negro Protest*. New York: Parents' Magazine Press, 1968.

Grant, Joanne (editor), *Black Protest*. New York: Fawcett, 1968.

Huie, William Bradford, *Three Lives for Mississippi*. New York: Signet-NAL, 1968.

King, Martin Luther, Jr., *Where Do We Go From Here?* New York: Harper & Row, 1967.

McGill, Ralph, *The South and the Southerners*. Boston: Atlantic Monthly Press, 1963.

Newfield, Jack, *A Prophetic Minority*. New York: New American Library, 1966.

X, Malcolm (with Alex Haley), *Autobiography of Malcolm X*. New York: Grove Press, 1964.

Zinn, Howard, *SNCC: The New Abolitionists*. Boston: Beacon Press, 1964.

ON THE ANTIWAR AND MC CARTHY MOVEMENTS

Frank, Joseph (editor), *The New Look In Politics*. Albuquerque: University of New Mexico Press, 1968.

Frost, David (editor), *The Presidential Debate*. New York: Stein & Day, 1968.

Mailer, Norman, *Armies of the Night*. New York: Signet-NAL, 1968.

McCarthy, Eugene, *The Year of the People*. New York: Doubleday, 1969.

Newfield, Jack, *Robert F. Kennedy; A Memoir*. New York: Dutton, 1969.

Schneir, Walter (editor), *Telling It Like It Was: The Chicago Riots*. New York: New American Library, 1969.

Wakefield, Dan, *Supernation at Peace and War*. New York: Bantam Books, 1968.
White, Theodore H., *The Making of the President, 1968*. New York: Atheneum, 1969.
Wicker, Tom, *JFK and LBJ*. New York: William Morrow, 1968.

ON THE STUDENT REVOLUTION

Avorn, Jerry (editor), *Up Against the Ivy Wall*. New York: Atheneum, 1969.
Kennan, George F., *Democracy and the Student Left*. Boston: Atlantic Monthly Press, 1968.
Lipset, Seymour M., and Wolin, Sheldon S. (editors), *The Berkeley Student Revolt*. New York: Doubleday, 1965.
Newfield, Jack, *A Prophetic Minority (Part II)*. New York: New American Library, 1966.

MAGAZINE AND NEWSPAPER ARTICLES
ON THE BLACK REVOLUTION (SNCC)

Liberation, January, 1970. "Mississippi: 1961-1962; Bob Moses."

ON THE ANTIWAR MOVEMENT

Christian Century, December 22, 1965. "Weighty Unanimity."
Commonweal, November 19, 1965. Editorial.
Harper's Magazine, April and May, 1969. "Nobody Knows . . . ," by Jerry Larner.
Life, December 10, 1965. Article on antiwar demonstrations in Oakland.
The Nation, August 22, 1966. "Selective Reprisal: Sniping at Dissent."
Newsweek, October 25, 1965. "Battle of Vietnam Day."
Newsweek, November 1, 1965. "Demonstrators, Why, How Many."
Newsweek, May 23, 1966. Article on college draft-exemption exams.
The New York Times Magazine, November 7, 1965. "Children in Line of March."
The New Yorker, December 11, 1965. Article by Renata Adler.
Readers' Digest, January 19, 1966. "Campus Demonstrations."
Readers' Digest, February, 1966. Reprint of *Life* article on draft system.
Saturday Review, December 18, 1965. "Burning Draft Cards."

ON THE MC CARTHY MOVEMENT

America, April 20, 1968. "We Do Our Thing for Gene," by Mary McGrory.

Business Week, July 6, 1968.

Life, March 22, 1968.

Life, March 29, 1968. Article by Hugh Sidney.

The New Republic, May 11, 1968. Article by Paul R. Wieck.

The New Republic, May 18, 1968. Article by Zalin B. Grant.

The New Republic, June 22, 1968. Article by Paul R. Wieck.

Saturday Review, May 18, 1968. "The Children's Crusade."

Time, March 22, 1968.

ON THE STUDENT REVOLUTION

Christian Century, February 12, 1969. "Black Studies Movement," by Richard L. Aukema.

Commonweal, January 31, 1969. Article by Nicholas von Hoffman.

Look, October 31, 1967. "Black Revolt Hits White Campus."

The Nation, January 8, 1968. "How to Wreck a Campus: Violence at San Francisco State."

The Nation, February 17, 1969. Article on Black Studies movement by Kenneth G. Gross.

Newsweek, February 10, 1969. Black Studies movement.

New York *Post*, May 20, 1969. City College Seminar.

The New York Times, May 4, 1969. Editorial on Amherst Declaration.

The New York Times, May 6, 1969. Black Studies story.

The New York Times Magazine, April 6, 1969. "The Black Studies Thing," by Ernest Dunbar.

Time, April 18, 1969. Harvard story.

INDEX

Draft cards, burning of, 68, 73, 74, 76
Draft resisters, 71, 72
"Dump Johnson" movement, 88, 89

Eisenhower administration, 13, 67
England, 73
Episcopal Peace Fellowship, 81
Equal Opportunities Program, 159, 162, 171
Esquire magazine, 120
Evers, Charles, 113, 173
Evers, Medgar, 41, 113, 173

Fayerweather Hall, Columbia Univ., 144
Fayette, Mississippi, 173
FBI, 45, 46, 53, 55, 88
Fisk University, 22
Ford Foundation, 159
Forman, James, 44, 58
France, 66
Freedom Riders, 27, 28, 31, 32
Freedom Rides, 27, 33
Freedom Schools, 38, 42, 50, 55, 70
Free Press, Washington, 84
Free Speech Movement, 132
Friedman, Robert, 135
Friends of Central Park, 140
Fromm, Erich, 151
Fulbright, Senator William (Arkansas), 73, 90

Galbraith, John Kenneth, 97
Gavin, General James, 90
Genet, Jean, 120
Germans, 72
Germany, Nazi, 41
Ghetto riots, 106, 140
Ghettos, 127, 135, 139, 155
Goodman, Andrew, 53, 55
Goodwin, Richard, 99, 124

Grant Park, Chicago, 119
Greene County, Alabama, 173
Greensboro, N.C., 19
Greenwood, Mississippi, 38
Grier, Roosevelt, 111
Gruening, Senator Ernest (Alaska), 70

Hamer, Mrs. Fannie Lou, 41, 51, 53, 56
Hamilton, Professor Charles, 158
Hamilton Hall, Columbia Univ., 142, 144, 145, 150
Hanoi, 96
Harlem, 61, 79, 135, 136, 138, 139, 140, 142, 144, 157
Harlem High School, 136
Harper's Magazine, 121
Hartke, Senator Vance (Indiana), 90
Harvard Corporation, 155
Harvard University, 68, 154, 155, 164
"Hawks," 73, 87
Hayes, Father, 81
Hershey, General Lewis B., 77
Hesburgh, Father, 154
Hilton Hotel, Chicago, 119
Hippies, 17, 70, 83, 134
Hirsch, Sy, 101
Hitler, Adolf, regime of, 72
Hoffman, Abbie, 81
House of Representatives, 92
Hoving, Thomas, 138, 140
Huie, William Bradford, 55
Humphrey, Hubert H., 56, 92, 102, 103, 106, 108, 109, 111, 113, 114, 115, 117, 118, 119, 124
Hurst, E. H., 35, 36

IBM, 136
IDA, 138, 139, 141, 142, 149, 150, 151, 153, 155

Making of the President 1968, The (White), 90

Manchester Guardian, 154

March on Washington, anti-Vietnam War (1967), 81

March on Washington, Civil Rights (1963), 48, 58, 81, 83

Marshall, Burke, 33

Marshall County, Mississippi, 39

Marshall Field Foundation, 33, 38

Massachusetts Institute of Technology, 153

Mathematics Hall, Columbia Univ., 144

McCarthy, Senator Eugene J. (Minnesota), 90, 91, 92, 93, 96, 97, 98, 99, 100, 101, 102, 103, 104, 106, 108, 109, 110, 111, 113, 114, 115, 117, 118, 120, 124, 152

McCarthy, Senator Joseph (Wisconsin), 13

McComb, Mississippi, 34, 35, 36, 38, 48

McGill, Ralph, 27

McGovern, Senator George (South Dakota), 90, 114, 117

McIntyre, Senator Thomas J. (New Hampshire), 93, 96

McKeithen, Governor John Julian (Louisiana), 163

McKissick, Floyd, 80

Memphis, Tennessee, 104, 111

Meredith, James, 59

Mexican-Americans, 110, 111

Michigan Selective Service, 77

Michigan, University of, 68

Military-industrial complex, 91, 127, 135, 152, 177

Milwaukee, Wisconsin, 99

Mississippi Constitution, 34

Mississippi Freedom Democratic Party, 51, 53, 56, 118

Mississippi Freedom Summer, 49, 80-81

Mississippi State Legislature, 35

Mississippi Summer Project, 49, 56, 70, 158

Mississippi, University of, 59

Mississippi voter-registration drive, 33, 37, 38, 42, 44, 49

Mobilization Committee to End the War in Vietnam, 115

Montgomery, Alabama, 14, 31, 32

Moratorium Day (October 15, 1969), 173

Morningside Heights, 135, 136, 137, 139, 140, 149

Morningside Heights Tenants' Action Committee, 149

Morningside Park, 135, 140, 151-2

Morse, Senator Wayne (Oregon), 73, 90

Moses, Robert Parris, 33-4, 35, 36, 37, 38, 55

NAACP, 21, 23, 31, 34, 38, 41, 42, 44, 49, 62

Napalm, 66, 68, 72, 74, 78, 139, 154

Nashville, Tennessee, 22

National Association for the Advancement of Colored People, *see* NAACP

National Committee for a Sane Nuclear Policy, *see* SANE

National Conference for the New Politics, *see* New Politics

National Council of Churches, 37, 49, 78

National Emergency Committee of Clergy Concerned About Vietnam, 78

National Guardian, 83-4

National Guardsmen, 32, 59, 81

National Mobilization to End the War in Vietnam, 81

National Selective Service Program, 77, 78, 88

National Student Association, 33, 88